A MASS ME[ETING]

of EAST END JEWS will be held

ON SUNDAY JULY 12th 1896 AT 6 P.M.

— AT THE —

JEWISH WORKINGMEN'S CLUB, GT. ALIE STREET, E.

to welcome

DR. THEODORE HERZL.

THE REV. DR. M. GASTER WILL PRESIDE

M. EPSTEIN, Hon. Sec. of Reception Committee

א מאסס מיטינג

ווירד געהאלטען ווערען אין דיא

דזואיש ווארקינגמענס קלוב, גרייט עלי סט. איסט

צו ווילקאמען דעם גרויסען וועלטבעריהמטען אידישען גאסט

דאקטער הערצל

רעדאקטאר פון דיא גרויסע דייטשע צייטונג „נייע פרייע פרעססע" מאן וויען
פערפאסער פון דעם געניאלען ווערק „דיא אידישע מדינה.

דיזען זאנטאג דען 12־טען דזוליי אום 6 אוהר אבענד

דאקטער הערצל קומט יעצט פון קאנסטאנטינאפל וואו ער האט געהאט איין
אוידיענין ביים סולטאן וועגען אבקויפען פאלעסטינא פיר דיא אידען. ער האט
דאצו אויך בעקומען דיא איינשטימונג פון פיעלע גרויסע אייראפעישע מיניסטערן.
דיעזער גרויסער מאן וועט ערשיינען זאנטאג אין דזואיש ווארקינגמענס קלוב און
וועט שצרערבען איבער זיינע וויכטיגע ארבייט און שטערעבונג פירס אידישע פאלק

רעוו. דר. מ. גאסטער וועט זיין אין דיא טשער.

דר. הערצל וועט שפרעכען אין ענגליש און דייטש.

גרויסע און אנגעוועהנליכע מעהנער פון אונזערע ענגלישע ברידער וועלן קומען צום מיטינג און
מאנכע פון וויא וועלען שפרעכען. מעראמט ניט דיא נילעגענהייט צו הערן דיעזען גרויסען מא...

דרוקערייא פון א.וו. ראבכינאוויטש, 64 היא סטריט וויטשעפעל.

HERZL'S JOURNEY

Conversations with a Zionist Legend

BERNARD ZISSMAN

DEVORA PUBLISHING
JERUSALEM ◆ NEW YORK

Also by Bernard Zissman

"A Knight out with Chamberlain"

Herzl's Journey: Conversations with a Zionist Legend
Published by Devora Publishing Company
Copyright © 2008 by Bernard Zissman. All rights reserved.

The right of Bernard Zissman to be identified as the author of this work has been asserted by him in accordance with the Copyright, Designs and Patents Acts 1988.

COVER DESIGN: Benjie Herskowitz
TYPESETTING & BOOK DESIGN: Koren Publishing Services
EDITOR: Sybil Ehrlich
EDITORIAL & PRODUCTION MANAGER: Daniella Barak

Hard Cover ISBN: 978-1-934440-23-0

E-MAIL: sales@devorapublishing.com
WEB SITE: www.devorapublishing.com

Printed in Israel

One thing is to me certain, high above any doubt: the movement will continue. I know not when I shall die, but Zionism will never die.

– Theodor Herzl

❧

This book is for my grandchildren:

Melissa, Sam, Alex, Vicki, Emily, Isabella and Jamie

with my prayers and hopes that they will grow up in a world
more at peace with itself than that of my generation.

❧

CONTENTS

LIST OF ILLUSTRATIONS

FOREWORD

By Dr Motti Friedman
Director of the Herzl Museum & Education Center Jerusalem

Theodor Herzl was one of the great personalities of Jewish history. He was born in an era of outstanding European culture and turbulent change. He devoted his short life to achieving the establishment of a Jewish national home in Palestine, a vision he was not to see realized in his time. *Herzl's Journey* tells the story of his exhausting travels in an innovative and easy style capturing the charm and excitement of the great cities of Europe including Basel, Paris and of course London and Vienna.

Reading this book about Bernard Zissman's conversations with Theodor Herzl has given me immense joy. The detailed descriptions of the meetings and events of the time represent an interesting insight into Herzl's life and achievements. The author's ability to walk the reader through the corridors of time and events is amazing, and as I read the pages I could picture myself so vividly by the side of Herzl in the restaurant or hotel lobby in Vienna or London, even in the audience of the First Zionist Congress in Basel.

Herzl's unique characteristics and charisma come alive throughout the book as the reader is given the feeling of actually being a part of the meetings.

Zissman introduces us to so many other characters of Jewish and Zionist history such as Max Nordau, Herzl's close ally whose addresses inspired Zionist Congresses; the outstanding English author Israel Zangwill; and the wealthy bankers and philanthropists Baron Hirsch and Baron Rothschild. In more recent times, we meet Chaim Weizmann, Israel's first president, and the legendary prime ministers Golda Meir and Yitzhak Rabin, as the author engages with Herzl capturing inspiring events across two centuries in an enlivening and interesting way.

I am sure that *Herzl's Journey* is a valuable asset to our generation. It is an important book which will enable a new and young generation to familiarize itself with Herzl, his vision and achievements. It should be read by everyone with an interest in the history of the region and certainly by every Jew.

PREFACE

I'm not sure why I decided to write this book. So much has already been written about Theodor Herzl by authors a great deal more informed than me and certainly more experienced in chronicling aspects of Jewish and Zionist history. So this book in no way sets out to mirror or compete with the excellent works already available, for they are all rich in fact and detail. It is perhaps just a story, of how someone who has lived through one of the most terrifying periods of world and Jewish history in the 1930s and '40s, witnessed the establishment of the State of Israel emerging from the horrors of that period, and then looks on as the peace for which everyone appears to hope and pray evades us all, particularly the Jewish and Arab peoples. It is inevitable that anything written about the Middle East, a saga in shifting sands, will always be out of date. What can never be out of date is how the saga began, how one man, Theodor Herzl, journeyed and struggled to bring about a dream. This book shares that journey and the amazing, and some may say miraculous, realization of that dream, the establishment of the State of Israel, and the sixty years which followed its birth.

The research for this book was undertaken almost exclusively by me and therefore any errors are mine alone. Inevitably, there are differences between biographers and historians in the interpretation of history, the spelling of names, and the matching of dates with locations.

Together with my greatest supporter and critic, my wife Cynthia, I travelled to Vienna, Basel, Israel and London, in pursuit of information and stories about Theodor Herzl. But nothing is achieved alone; I have received encouragement, advice and practical help from so many friends and contacts. In Vienna I was helped by our cherished friend Alex Gertner, who, with typical generosity, provided Viennese background and introduced me to Elisabet Torggler of the Vienna Jewish Museum. I am grateful to Victor Gray, director of the Rothschild Archives, who provided valuable material, and to Frau Katia Guth-Dreyfus of the Jewish Museum of Switzerland in Basel, whose knowledge of the Zionist Congresses was so helpful, as were the books she provided.

Throughout preparation of this book I have received good advice and help from friends in Israel: Marcia Lewison, Daniella and David Cohen and their family, and especially Ora and Milton Perlman, who not only read my manuscript with critical eyes, but helped me to better understand the feelings of the original Israeli *chalutzim* (pioneers). I was lucky to meet Mohammad Darawshe, who provided an insight into the Arab perspective. Dr. Motti Friedmann, director of the Herzl Museum and Education Center in Jerusalem, loaned me a number of photographs from his personal collection, generously gave time to offer valued advice and review my early manuscript, suggesting changes and challenging me to "think again". Closer to home, I have received continual encouragement from friends who may have tired with the time it has taken to write this book, yet still gave help. Esther Schott, who listened patiently to the closing chapters and added a different aspect to my conclusion; Tony Travis and Nicole Newman for lending me excellent books of reference; Ruth and Leo Cohen for being mines of information and for their ability to translate; and finally, in sadness, the late Joy Pond, a courageous friend for proof reading my earlier manuscript. I reserve special thanks for my editors. Bob Mullan, whom I stumbled across accidentally and who shared my enthusiasm, providing invaluable input as well as editing and correcting the manuscript. Finally to Sybil Ehrlich, my Israeli editor who painstakingly checked every page, correcting and questioning. As a result of their efforts, the book will be better understood and is certainly more accurate and readable.

I suppose I had the urge, a rather impossible urge, to meet the founder of Zionism, and after all, wasn't it Herzl himself who said "if you will it, it is no dream"? I have endeavored to respect the accuracy of historical dates and events and trust the reader will forgive where, in the interests of the flow of the story, I have taken some liberty with the sequence of some of those events. This book is, after all, a story. I hope it will inspire younger generations to have a better understanding of the Zionist cause and how and why the State of Israel came about. I hope it will inspire them to continue the search for peace, something which, as I write this book, has evaded my generation.

So let us dream together. I wanted to understand what drove Herzl to create his vision of a Jewish national home and why it had to be in Palestine. Was it just the impact of anti-Semitism in Paris and the world-famous Dreyfus case, or some other experience? Why only a hesitancy of compromise about the exact location of this new state? What would he have felt about the modern State of Israel? This book is for everyone to read, particularly the younger generations, be they Jew or non-Jew, for both need to understand what drove Zionist leaders such as Theodor Herzl and those who followed him to strive for a Jewish national home. Now that it exists we must emulate his energy, diplomacy and vision to bring about a peace in the Middle East, so that all those who live there with their own dreams can call the land a national home. I have struggled to understand who precisely the "Palestinians" are. All of the evidence suggests it was never an Arab country, their leaders claim it had no biblical reference and all of the organizations associated with Palestine have been Jewish. So why has so much effort been made to change history by inferring that Palestinian refugees are all Arabs?

Throughout history, the Jewish people have always been united in a feeling of persecution and distress. Despite the happiness and joy of so many individual occasions, it is our tears that have bound us together. The tragic period of the Holocaust has touched every Jewish family throughout the world, many at first hand, others more distantly. It was another example of how distress kept our people united and strong enough to survive until the next set of tears. The emergence of the modern State of Israel in 1948 wasn't just a realization of Herzl's dream; it answered the aspirations and hopes of most Jews – certainly not *all* Jews – wherever they lived throughout the world. I can't help wondering if Herzl could have realized his dream a hundred years earlier how many millions of Jews might have been saved.

As a Jew and Zionist myself, I wondered if I could write a book which showed no natural bias. Could I be dispassionate about the conflict between Arab and Jew and write the final chapter, which might just have sufficient integrity to motivate new thoughts and change the way both sides to the dispute would think in the future?

Bernard Zissman
November 2007

PROLOGUE

"The captain has now switched on the seat belt sign. Will you please fasten your seat belt, make sure that your seat is in the upright position and your table stowed…"

As the words floated in Hebrew through the cabin of the El Al Boeing 737, which bore the name *Jerusalem* on its fuselage, and were repeated in English, I sat quietly by the window looking out at the green landscape which was rushing up towards us. My thoughts were interrupted by a further announcement.

"We have just landed at Ben-Gurion Airport. Please remain seated until the aircraft has come to a complete stop and the seat belt signs have been switched off. Please take particular care when opening the overhead compartments. On behalf of Captain Levy and the crew I thank you for choosing to fly with El Al. We wish you a happy visit and welcome you to Israel, where the local time in Tel Aviv is 5:45 in the afternoon. *Shalom*."

As we taxied, I listened to the light classical music which filled the cabin as the passengers girded themselves to jump from their seats to stand in the aisle whilst they waited, cramped and uncomfortable, for the doors to be opened, as if they might be left behind. Listening to the music, I recalled how, in years gone by, we'd have been greeted by vibrant Israeli songs of welcome, perhaps *Hevenu Shalom Aleichem*. It seemed that the Jews felt the need to be more like everyone else.

Around me, the passengers represented a United Nations in the flesh – skins of various colors and shades; men, women and children whose range of age, appearance and variety of dress gave the impression that we were traveling through history in this machine in the sky. Some wore jeans and flimsy T-shirts hardly disguising the odd tattoo on a bare female shoulder. All had a look of expectancy of their impending arrival in this land, still reflecting a spirit of hope and opportunity to be a pioneer. Mingling with them, mothers and fathers, grandmothers and grandfathers, most with a look of excitement in their eyes at the prospect of once again seeing their beloved children and grandchildren.

Standing out from the crowd were the Orthodox Jewish men, young and old, with pale faces, all with wide-brimmed black hats, from which dropped ringlets of hair. Most were clutching precious boxes, retrieved from the overhead lockers in which were their Shabbat hats. They were dressed traditionally, in black coats, with a simple belt keeping the coat neatly in place and below which could occasionally be spied the fringes of their *tzitzit* worn by all Orthodox Jewish men as a reminder of their religious commitment.

And of course there were the Israeli passengers returning home from working or holidaying abroad. Most appeared to be tall, handsome or beautiful, bronzed and with a look of determination, even defiance, totally at odds with the outdated images of the bent, hook-nosed and cringing Jews of Eastern Europe, each one was determined to be the first off the plane.

It was a bright and warm afternoon, the sun casting its glow upon this small land at the crossroads where the cultures of the East and West merged. Sitting in the back of the car as it sped along the road from Tel Aviv to Jerusalem, I looked around and observed the people going about their business preparing to return home at the end of a hard day in the hot sun – Arabs, now wearing western dress having given up the traditional white flowing robes of their parents, mingling with Jews, many with traditional *kippot,* skullcaps in a variety of designs and colors and dressed in T-shirts and shorts.

The final word of the stewardess continued to ring in my ears. *Shalom*, a word which had a hundred meanings from hello to goodbye, a word when translated literally into English means *peace*, which had somehow eluded these people for over fifty years.

Our car arrived at the outskirts of Jerusalem in the dying moments of the day's sun as it reflected on the domes and structures of some of the world's great places of worship, the Dome of the Rock, Al-Aqsa Mosque, the Church of the Holy Sepulchre, the Great Synagogue and the Western Wall of the Second Temple.

I had a simple mission here; to visit Mount Herzl, the final resting place of a man who had lived for just forty-four years, and whose vision had been the foundation of the State of Israel.

It was late in the day and my task would have to wait. The car pulled up into the slight incline of the semicircular drive and stopped outside the impressive front door of the King David, one of the world's great hotels. The door was opened by a top-hatted doorman, and I stepped into the reception lobby surrounded by walls which had witnessed history in the making and had hosted world leaders from East and West.

That night, as I looked from my window on the fourth floor, I gazed out onto splendid gardens and beyond, to the Old City of Jerusalem. It wasn't difficult to understand the fervency and determination of those who wished to claim this unique city as their own. Reflecting over 3,000 years of the history of the world, it breathed the story of mankind in every building and street, in every tree and every flower. The City of David and Solomon, where the world began, where Abraham, the father of three great peoples, was sent by God to sacrifice his son, and where Jesus had walked and Muhammad had allegedly ascended to heaven.

I could not help but wonder at the madness which now dominates the lives of these people, whether Jew or Arab, locked in a war which has lasted sixty years, both robbed of so many fine young men, women and children who had never had the chance to live.

*   *   *

I stood at the grave of one of the greatest personalities in Jewish history.

As I strolled slowly and thoughtfully between the bushes of contrasting greens, rose bushes, a variety of flowers, taking in the scent of the lilac and lavender, until reaching a wide walkway overlooked on each side by twelve flagpoles, as if keeping a watchful eye on the occupant and which opened up onto a wide esplanade. I could smell the fragrance of the petunias and geraniums in various shades of reds and pinks. Behind the tomb was a semicircular construction resembling a spider's web, made from tubular scaffolding and with seats for those who might wish to sit and contemplate. Somehow, I thought the style out of place in this quiet, peaceful and solemn spot.

It was not a depressing location, although it was a memorial to other members of the Herzl family and some of the great leaders of the Jewish people, including the great Zionist activist Ze'ev Jabotinsky, and the former prime minister Yitzhak Rabin, who might have had the hope of peace in the Middle East in his grasp before his cruel assassination.

At the far end stood a square, black granite tomb on a plinth, within a simple, circular garden, on which were inscribed the four Hebrew letters הרצל, Herzl.

This was the place on Mount Herzl in the City of Jerusalem where the remains of Theodor Herzl had been brought in 1949 from Vienna where he had died some forty-five years earlier, at the untimely age of forty-four. Here was where the man described as the founder of the Zionist movement and the visionary of the Jewish State lay.

Theodor Herzl, born in 1860, a man who looked so much older than his forty-four short but full years. A man who had traveled across Europe from his birthplace in Budapest to Vienna, from Paris to London, and from Istanbul to Jerusalem.

I sat quietly looking at this simple tomb, and thinking about this man and what might have been.

I'm not sure how long I sat there, but the peaceful atmosphere was disturbed only by a white butterfly which fluttered above and contrasted sharply with the black granite of the tomb. It was October, a week or so after the Jewish harvest festival of Sukkot or Tabernacles, and the end of the period of the High Holy Days. It was the ninth month of the Islamic calendar, Ramadan, the holiest in the Muslim calendar; the month of fasting and the strengthening of family and community ties around the evening meal of *iftar*. The afternoon was warm, with few people about, and the gardens, somewhat dry, seemed sorry to see the end of the summer, yet hoping for the relief of some rain to come. Again I thought, what if…

Life is always so full of "what ifs". What if Herzl had lived another forty-four years? What would he have thought in 1948 as the State of Israel was born? What if he had been spared to live 120 years, in accordance with the traditional Jewish wish for long life? And so my mind began to wander back a century or so. If, just if, I could have met this man…

PART ONE
THE DREAM

CHAPTER ONE

Vienna, Austria, 1890

It was May 1890. I was sitting in a fairly worn but comfortable leather armchair in the study of a modest apartment in Stephansplatz, in the city of Vienna. Sitting opposite me, behind an elegant and equally worn dark mahogany desk, was a youngish man, whose age was disguised by a sizable square black beard which covered his shirt collar although his bow tie just peeped out. It was clear from the cut of his frock coat that his style of dress was important to him. It was hard to believe that he'd just celebrated his thirtieth birthday.

"Thank you, Dr. Herzl, for seeing me so promptly," I said, quietly, for this was indeed the man destined to become one of the greatest visionaries among the Jewish people, a man who wrote himself into the history books.

"Thank you, Herr Zissman, for making the journey to meet me." As he spoke, he held up a piece of paper. "I found your letter fascinating and have been anxious to see you to discuss life in England."

I wanted the conversation to continue and sought for some well-chosen words, hoping that what I was about to say wouldn't sound too trivial. "May I congratulate you and Mrs. Herzl on the birth of your daughter, and may I ask what name you've given her?"

"Indeed, you may," came the reply, which seemed tinged with a mixture of delight and sadness. "We've called her Pauline, and you must meet her and her mother during your visit."

I realized why his response had been given in such a tone. The new baby had been named after Herzl's sister Pauline, who had tragically died of typhoid some twelve years earlier in her nineteenth year.

"You'll stay for some light supper and then explain why you're so anxious to talk to me," he said, as he rose from his chair. He looked at me with just a little puzzlement, but not yet ready to question the difference in our dress or my strange appearance. I felt it would be almost impossible to tell him about how I'd stood in front of his tomb more than a century later in Jerusalem and dreamed of the opportunity to meet him.

He excused himself and left the room to ask his wife to prepare supper. I looked around the study and could see from the range of books and the open manuscripts on the desk that he was probably well read; certainly a writer of some kind. Among the papers were sheets of handwritten music suggesting that Herzl was writing a musical score, possibly the libretto for an operetta. It seemed very Viennese. I suppose the certificate in the elegant frame on top of the bookcase confirming that Theodor Herzl was a member of the Vienna Union of Journalists should have convinced me of his profession. I was not being inquisitive, just interested, and I could see an open copy of a newspaper, *Berliner Tageblatt*, with an article by Herzl. In answer to a later question he told me that this was one of a regular series of articles he wrote for the German paper about the social and cultural life of Vienna. On the wall was a framed picture of what appeared to be a lovely house in some mountainous location, and I made a mental note to ask Herzl where this picture was taken.

I thought about the journey which had brought me to Vienna from London. At London Bridge Station I'd boarded a steam train, painted in the livery of the South Eastern Railway Company, for the journey which had taken about two days. We traveled to Folkestone and here I'd booked to join one of the steamships, *Ajax*, which would carry me across the English Channel to Boulogne, where I would connect with the train to Paris.

I was dreading the Channel crossing. I'm not a good sailor and the reputation of the English Channel had made me feel worse. It wasn't unusual for many passengers to be seasick and for me to be the first in the queue. The fear of being shipwrecked and the chance of the engine breaking down were quite high. It wasn't unknown for ferries to be unable to enter the harbor due to the tides and choppy sea, particularly at nearby Calais, and passengers were then tempted into smaller boats to complete their journey. Fortunately, I reached Boulogne safely, with only some minor sickness and was extremely pleased to feel firm land underfoot.

Before my train left Boulogne for Paris, I walked for a few moments on the platform and took some light refreshment. We were due in Paris that evening and would travel through the night to reach Vienna the following morning.

My thoughts about the interesting travel experience were interrupted by the reappearance of Herzl, who came into the room followed by a younger woman whom I presumed to be Julie, his wife. She was dressed simply, but elegantly, in a striped v-necked dress to her ankles with a high-necked blouse and gathered sleeves. Her dark curly hair was neatly piled on top of her head.

"Herr Zissman, may I present Frau Herzl who, if you don't object, will join us for a light supper in the drawing room." I stood and bowed slightly and took the slender hand offered to me by the elegant and attractive lady. "It's my pleasure. I didn't intend for you to be put to any trouble in offering me hospitality," I replied.

Herzl stood by the open door and, with a sweeping hand, indicated that we should move to the adjoining room. I could hear the light strains of a Strauss waltz from the newly invented gramophone in the corner as we moved to sit around the table on which were a cream embroidered cloth and some elegant china and cutlery. There was a range of dishes on which were displayed black and brown breads, cheeses and fruit cake, all of which smelled good and looked even better. Two decanters containing wine and a cut-glass jug of water completed the offering. Julie Herzl was a fine hostess as she offered the food first to me and then to her husband.

As we sat at the table, I noticed the sepia pictures on the sideboard of two groups, clearly family portraits and probably his parents, Jacob and Jeanette Herzl, and his parents-in-law, Jacob and Johanna Naschauer. I was a little surprised to see a pair of silver candlesticks and an elegant eight- branched *menorah,* the symbolic candelabrum of Hanukkah. Herzl noticed my glance and smiled, "I know what you're thinking, Herr Zissman, I'm not well known for my strong religious belief."

"Please excuse me," I replied with some embarrassment, for, whilst I was well aware of his lack of commitment to Orthodoxy, I had no doubt about his commitment to Judaism and a deep feeling of belonging. "If we're to spend a little time together perhaps you might care to call me Bernard..."

Herzl stared at me with a strange look, accompanied by a smile, "We'll see about that." I realized that I shouldn't confuse a formality of address with a desire to be unfriendly. Herzl managed to ease the formal atmosphere without the convenience of first names.

Herzl thought for a few moments as he took a small amount of cheese and began to eat slowly. He lifted his glass, which had been filled with a red wine, and took a few sips. "My parents were not Orthodox Jews. I suppose you might have called them traditional, although both Julie's and my grandparents were strictly observant. I was born in the house next door to the Tabakgasse Synagogue, which opened in the year of my birth. My parents were well aware of the laws and customs they'd been Orthodoxy brought up with, and When we moved here to Vienna, the circles in which they mixed were moving away from Judaism. They ceased to practice its tenets, and became assimilated in the wider community."

It didn't appear appropriate to interrupt, so I let him continue.

"You might consider this all the more surprising when I tell you that despite living within a fairly small community at the time, my grandfather Simon was appointed by Rabbi Alcalai to lead the congregation in the *Kol Nidre* prayer (which introduces the Yom Kippur service). He was give the honor of blowing the *shofar* (the traditional ram's horn at the High Holy Day services)." Herzl smiled momentarily before continuing, "I met a great deal of anti-Semitism at university, as well as socially; indeed I even suspect that I may have had a touch of anti-Semitism in me," he said with a wry smile, "and I felt that being Jewish was hardly going to advance my career."

I was mildly shocked by this admission. I might have thought ill of him if I hadn't had the benefit of knowing what Herzl was to later become, and how he was to change so dramatically his attitude to his forebears. Against a background of some Jews wanting to disappear "into the crowd", Herzl was destined to stand out. He wanted to ensure that Jews would be widely accepted, and he questioned whether assimilation was the answer. But for someone who had become so assimilated in the Western European way of life and devoid of the Eastern European culture of his people, I couldn't help but be amazed that his return to the Jewish people was to have such an impact on their future and those of generations to follow.

"I was greatly influenced by my early years studying law at Vienna University. I had become, you may say, somewhat foolishly, a member of Albia, a right-wing nationalist organization which I left because of the anti-Semitism of its members. At about the same time the world-famous composer Richard Wagner died, and the people went into what appeared to me a period of national mourning, something I could not associate myself with as I felt the quality of his music was tainted by his fanatical anti-Semitism. He was honored by everyone, no more so than by the Union of German Students here in Vienna, and actively supported by Albia. It didn't take me long to realize that denying one's heritage didn't automatically free one from being the victim of racist aggression."

He stopped talking, as if in deep thought, and began again to eat, anticipating that I might want to respond. I sensed a degree of soul searching in my host, a kind of coming to terms with the fact that he'd turned his back on his roots.

"You shouldn't be too harsh on yourself," I replied quietly. "If the roots of your heritage have been planted firmly, in time they'll grow and you may yet return to become an inspiration to others."

Herzl looked at me in surprise as I continued. "One thing I've learned in life is that in whatever direction our fellow Jews turn, never underestimate the strength of a Jewish heart, which ultimately is the driving force of body and mind."

Julie Herzl had been listening with discreet attention and the lull in our conversation encouraged her to intervene and invite us to partake of some further refreshment. Although I'd eaten enough already, it seemed somewhat rude, if not ungracious, to refuse some of the delicious-looking strudel, which she modestly admitted was home-made. My protest at the size of the portion fell on the deaf ears of a typical Jewish hostess.

Herzl seemed to gain some fresh enthusiasm to talk, and as we finished our meal he wiped his mouth and beard on his pristine napkin and said, "Let's retire to the study and then you can tell me about good old England and the purpose of your visit."

As we rose, Frau Herzl said, "Theodor, I'll bring you some coffee and perhaps you'll open that fine cognac you've been saving and even smoke a cigar – but please confine that to your study." We both smiled at this comment as we left for the adjoining room.

We went back into the study and this time Herzl joined me, having poured two goblets of cognac. As I've always claimed to be merely a social drinker a small brandy didn't seem inconsistent. The cigar, however, I did decline, without any feeling of embarrassment.

"When you wrote to me asking for this meeting, you said that you had some firm objectives in mind. Perhaps you could explain?"

I paused before answering. Although I'd anticipated this question and rehearsed what I might say, I was anxious that Herzl would not regard me as eccentric or even worse, unbalanced by my presumed powers of foresight.

"I'm eager to get to know you and understand you, Dr. Herzl, for fate has a strange way of working. We're nearing the end of a great century, a unique period in history, and I'd like to discuss its impact on the Jewish people. Perhaps we can project ourselves forward and imagine what the future has to offer, how the twentieth century will treat us and who might emerge to become an inspiration for our people – a shining beacon of vision and leadership, someone who could change the map of the world."

Herzl glanced at me over the top of his brandy goblet but made no immediate comment on what he must have considered to be wild speculation; and whether he'd been wise to invite me into his home.

"Zissman, my friend, you've set us an ambitious target, if not an exciting one. Let's sleep on it and tomorrow we'll walk about this city, talk of its history, see its fine buildings and have a drink in one of its cafes. To put it in your words, we'll get to know each other. Would that appeal to you?"

"Indeed it would," I replied quickly, "I've heard Vienna described as a city of peaceful parks with elegant streets in an environment of civilized behavior."

Herzl laughed as he replied, "Quite so. Our people are friendly, if not a little reserved, and certainly very proud."

CHAPTER TWO

Vienna, Austria, 1890

It was a bright crisp morning in May as Herzl and I left his home in Stephansplatz to walk around Vienna. I was looking forward to the experience even though I was beginning to struggle as to how I might explain the exact purpose of my visit.

The contrast in our dress drew some attention. Herzl, elegantly dressed in a black frock coat, shiny shoes and equally shiny silk top hat, blended well with the environment, whereas my dress seemed somewhat anachronistic.

"Vienna is one of the truly great cities of Europe, if not the world," said Herzl as his silver-topped cane tapped on the cobblestone footpath. He appeared similar in height to me, perhaps a couple of inches shorter, although his hat gave him a distinct advantage. We walked in step, as he continued speaking. "It is a city of outstanding culture, a city of music and architecture, the envy of so many other cities, yet not a perfect city…" He seemed to move into a daydream, giving me an opportunity to respond.

"What brought your family to Vienna from Budapest?" I asked. "Was the move of benefit to you and your family?"

"I was born in Pest, which my father used to say was on the better side of the Danube which divided us from Buda," he replied with a laugh, "and which, of course, is now known as Budapest. I came here with my parents in 1878, Julie followed and, yes, it's been a good move. By the time we arrived in Vienna, Jews had been enjoying full citizenship rights for about ten or eleven years. I benefited from a good education at the University of Vienna; my mind has been challenged and is full of questions, and some answers. I suppose I've been granted the gift of the pen and how to use it." I took this to mean that he believed he had an ability to write.

It was a short walk to the junction of Stephansplatz and Kärntner Strasse, where we turned to look at the imposing sight of St. Stephen's Cathedral.

"This outstanding building is at the heart of Vienna," said Herzl. "Its elegant spire rises over 130 meters and the cathedral dates back 570 years. Make sure you go inside, my friend, and look at the stained-glass windows which reflect Jewish life at the time of its building." He took my arm and pointed to Kärntner Strasse. "We'll walk down this street and I'll introduce you to the unique delights of the coffee shops of Vienna. We'll stop at the Sacher Hotel, which was completed about fourteen years ago. I'm confident its splendor will outlive our generation and those that follow."

As we left the Stephansplatz I glanced back at the cathedral, with its ornate roof; Herzl wasn't alone in his admiration of the structure.

There was a bustle about the place, resplendent with elegant ladies, wearing hats and long dresses in creams and beiges. Men strolled up and down the street, many dressed in coats below the knee, some with bow ties, others with high collars and huge knotted cravats, and few, if any, without either a silk top hat or high bowler hat. The younger men sported straw boaters and knickerbockers, which I associated with plus-fours, though I doubted many had ever played golf. A streetcar rumbled past with the driver standing in an exposed front cab, as if prepared to shout a warning to any trespasser who might walk in front. Passing us in the opposite direction was a horse-drawn cab with two upright gentlemen as passengers. I was walking by the edge of the pavement and jumped aside to avoid a trundling cart overflowing with sacks of grain or potatoes.

One thing which struck me was the number of bicycles. "Tell me, Doctor, do you ride a bicycle?"

"I do not," came the quick reply, "the city's already so overcrowded that the City Council has introduced regulation, although I don't know *what* they regulate," he smirked, with a smile slightly hidden by his beard.

We walked on down Kärntner Strasse and Herzl pointed out the interesting buildings and the fine sculpture which appeared the hallmark of Vienna. I looked up at No. 2, with elegant windows behind well-crafted metal balustrades, rising some four stories and in line with the adjoining buildings. Some of the balustrades were finished with white lamp shades which I imagined would add to the elegance of the street at night. Herzl continued his commentary as we walked, and now and again he touched his hat in recognition of a passerby and seemed to display a special twinkle in his eye when an attractive lady lowered her head in his direction.

We passed by Neuer Markt with its central statue dominating the square and paused outside the Maltese Church. I glanced inside this small sanctuary with its impressive painting sitting between two stained glass windows, one of which contained a Maltese cross. Further along on the left we passed Johannesgasse, a narrow street which led down to the Stadtpark. I was fascinated by the street traders, some hauling carts, others with their wares in trays slung around their necks. We entered another imposing square with a dramatic building which cast a shadow across the whole area. Herzl preempted my question. "That is the State Opera House. We'll take our coffee here in Philharmonikerstrasse at the Sacher Hotel. I am sure there will be other guests who'll equally interest you."

It seemed that the coffee and cake wouldn't be the only delights I would experience.

The front doors were opened by a uniformed doorman, who bade us good morning. We strolled through the lobby, a small area which was dominated by a rather over-large chandelier, which sparkled from regular cleaning. We paused by the entrance of the lounge around which sat some of the finest of Viennese society; the elder men elegant in dark dress coats and striped trousers, and the younger ones dressed in shades of brown and light gray. They outnumbered the chic ladies, all of whom wore hats in a variety of shades and designs carefully chosen to blend with their beautiful dresses. They displayed the fashion of the period, dominated by the bustle and oversized sleeves. Waiters glided between the tables, quietly depositing pots of coffee or chocolate, accompanied by plates of small cakes and almonds.

Leaving the lounge we walked down a corridor until we reached Sacherstube, a small and intimate café where most of the tables were occupied by the local Viennese, drinking from minute china cups. The maitre d'hotel, formally dressed in dark gray morning coat, striped trousers, white shirt with a wing collar and gray cravat, bowed slightly, and with a sweep of his arm beckoned us to follow him to a window table.

"*Guten Tag*, Dr. Herzl, it's good to see you again. I trust you are well."

"Indeed I am, Manfred." It was clear that Herzl was a frequent visitor.

The menu, decorated with butterflies and winged waiters, which I presumed indicated the speed of the service, was placed in front of us. I looked carefully down the list seeking not just something I would enjoy but actually understand. My host was aware of my problem and suggested that we try a cup of the house coffee with a slice of strudel or even the specialty of the hotel, a piece of Sachertorte. "Coffee and strudel would be fine for me," I said, and Herzl ordered, "*Zwei Kaffee, ein Strudel und eine Torte, bitte.*"

I turned to look out of the window at the magnificent Opera

House. "I expect you'd like to visit the opera while you're in Vienna?" questioned Herzl. "Yes, I would."

He leaned over the table towards me. "You see those two tables either side of the door?" he continued. "Sitting with the group of three men is Solomon Buber with his son, Martin. I doubt if Herr Buber is eating anything here because he's not only a famous scholar of the scriptures but is totally observant of Jewish dietary laws."

The mention of Martin Buber's name brought instant recognition to me, for only with the benefit of foresight could I know that he was destined to become a great Zionist, and savior of so many Jews suffering under German domination in the First World War before eventually settling in Palestine.

My thoughts were interrupted by Herzl, glancing in the direction of the other table where a man sat alone: "That is Sigmund Freud; he's a story in himself. I'll try and introduce you to him if possible."

I couldn't believe that I was sitting amongst such influential Jewish giants of European history.

"Tell me of your time here in Vienna and about your writings. I couldn't help but notice some of the transcripts on your desk. What's influenced you, and how do you see your future?"

He thought for a moment during which the coffee and cake arrived. They were served by a waitress in a pure white uniform, complete with cap and white gloves, who placed a silver coffee pot, sugar bowl and milk jug in front of us. The strudel and torte were served on a two-tier silver stand and the serving was completed with coffee spoons and cake forks. I had to admire the style and elegance, which sadly was to disappear from many cafés as the years passed.

"This afternoon I'll show you the university where I gained my law degree and where I encountered my first experience of serious anti-Semitism. But first, let's take in the atmosphere of this place and you can tell me why you've made the journey to see me."

I thought for a few moments, heeding Herzl's advice as I glanced around the café and tried to imagine what the other guests were talking about, here at the heart of the Hapsburg Empire.

"Yesterday, you'll recall that, apart from seeking to know and understand you better, I wanted to explore with you how the next century might treat our people, and quite rightly, you expressed the view that this was ambitious."

Herzl looked at me and replied quietly, "I suspect by the term 'our people' you mean the Jewish people. Why do you think that I, Theodor Herzl, not the most observant Jew, nor even religious, who once nearly embraced the opportunity of baptism, might help you in this objective?" It was indeed a fair question that deserved an answer, but how could I admit to having knowledge of later times without being dismissed as some sort of lunatic?

"Dr. Herzl, you're a man of considerable talent, highly educated and professionally qualified. Beyond that, I imagine you to be a man of vision, who hasn't yet even begun to realize his potential. You have the rare skill of the use of words in a style that can convince others and achieve victory in any debating arena."

Herzl sipped his coffee as he quizzically listened. I was unsure if this was from a sense of modesty or mere disbelief. "I'm not yet convinced, my English friend, but you fascinate me. Do please continue."

"First, let's continue our tour of Vienna. Show me where you benefited from the fine education you mentioned earlier, take me on an exploration of the great architectural assets of the city, help me understand its history so that I may have a better feeling for why this city – perhaps more than any other in the whole of Europe – seems to harbor so much dislike, even hatred for Jews, despite what they've done for Austria." It would be difficult, at this time, to have predicted how the future of Jewish life would develop in Vienna and the country of which it was the capital.

"So, where would you like to start? We're some way from the university but we can walk across the city, if you feel able, and I'll explain the significance of some of the buildings we pass."

"There's one building that I'd particularly like to see: the synagogue. I think it's on Seitenstettengasse," I managed to stutter.

Herzl smiled at my difficulty with German. "You know we've over forty synagogues in Vienna, and I cannot honestly admit that I'm familiar with *any* of them. You may also wish to see the Leopoldstadt Temple, which is relatively new, in historical terms, and completed about thirty years ago."

"Sounds good to me," I nodded, with some surprise at his knowledge of buildings he rarely visited. "We can talk as we walk," I added.

He signaled to a passing waiter that we required the bill, and as he rose to retrieve our coats, he again looked in the direction of the corner tables. "Tomorrow, we'll visit the Burgtheater. I've a surprise there for you, and to complete the evening we'll share some supper with an enlightened group of Viennese Jews – born in or adopted by our city."

In answer to my questioning look, he took my arm and steered me to the door as we stepped out on to the Ringstrasse. I felt a deep sense of excitement that I was about to start a journey of enlightenment, not open to any ordinary visitor to Vienna.

*   *   *

The sun was still shining as we began walking along Opernring and I noticed the billboard outside the Opera House which advertised an operetta by Johann Strauss, *Die Fledermaus*, to be conducted by the Maestro himself. I glanced at Herzl, who was already reading my mind. "I'll endeavor to obtain some tickets, if you'd like to see one of Strauss's finest works. My wife has expressed some admiration for his music and he's still the toast of the whole of Austria."

"As I admitted earlier, I cannot think of an experience I'd like more here in Vienna," I replied, as we continued our walk along the road which encircled the Innere Stadt, the old town center. We passed several street musicians and it appeared to my untrained ear that they played with considerable skill.

"These musicians are, sadly, regarded as beggars," commented Herzl. "Many are Jewish and they're among the best in the whole of Austria."

I couldn't help wondering what great violinists I might be hearing playing in the street.

We'd reached Burgring, and the joyful voices of children playing in the Burggarten could be heard over the passing carriages rolling along the cobbled streets. Suddenly we came to another example of Vienna's fine buildings which Herzl quickly informed me was the House of Parliament. "This has been an outstanding century of innovative construction and design which I doubt will be repeated." He was of course right. Building after building, sculpture after sculpture, seemed to emerge as we walked along the Ringstrasse, and their beauty seemed enhanced by the sun gently slipping behind the buildings. "Just look over there, beyond the park, that's the new Town Hall. We call it the Rathaus, just seven years since its completion, and those eight statues immortalize Viennese notables, including the town's rabbi.

"I plan to take you tomorrow night to the Burgtheater," which with a gesture of his arm, he pointed out as we passed by, "because they'll be performing my play, *The Fugitive*, which I wrote last year. There were some who didn't think it an outstanding piece of work, I have to tell you, but fear not, it's only one act," said Herzl, with a smile.

"Pray tell me, how much weight was placed on these critics?"

"That's indeed an interesting question. The principal critic was Ernst Hartmann, who was himself a well-known actor in Vienna and who I'd hoped would play the leading part. Alas, he wasn't enthusiastic and refused to appear on stage, but to my immense relief he agreed to direct the play and it opened last year to reasonable acclaim. I have to be content with the Burgtheater's agreement to perform it just once this year and, hopefully, for some years to come."

Walking onwards we came to another sturdy edifice.

"What is this building?" I inquired.

"That, my friend, is the Parliament building and beyond the Rathauspark is the University of Vienna, where I graduated just six years ago. In fact, I'd started my university education at the old university which we'll see tomorrow, but this building before you is truly magnificent. Let's look inside for just a moment or two."

We went through some large double doors and the impact of the wide center court with a stunning staircase took one's breath away. "This is truly magnificent."

"Yes, it is. It took eleven years to construct, but its effect on the students is dynamic and the quality of the structure is excelled only by the quality of the tutors."

As we reached the street, Herzl beckoned to a passing cab. "We'll ride home; dusk is approaching and before long there'll be a chill in the air."

Although the sky was darkening, I looked up at the street lights and realized that they were powered by electricity and not gas. "How long has Vienna had electric lighting?" I asked.

He thought for a moment before replying, "Only within the last few years, and it's made a big difference to the streets."

I'd sensed a feeling of pride as he spoke of his time at the university, although I also detected a touch of doubt which was difficult to gauge. "You seem to have mixed feelings about your stay at the university," I said quietly.

"I'm sorry to say that education was not the only thing I experienced there." I looked at him inquiringly. "It was there that I met anti-Semitism, which I've found deeply rooted in Viennese society. It is, in my view, a tragedy that a city with such a history and so much greatness about it also seems to be so anxious to discriminate against Jews. I often ask myself, where will it end?"

I couldn't help but speculate on the future. What major event in European history would trigger the mind of this visionary man to respond to the antagonism which seemed traditionally to be felt by the people on whom he had, in his early days, turned his back? I wondered what force lay slumbering in this man destined for such a role in Jewish history. I looked at him and at the strong features of his face and the firmness of his step. Did he realize what lay in store for him before the century would close?

* * *

Herzl had been true to his word. The tickets for the opera were produced and together with him and his wife I attended the performance of *Die Fledermaus*. It was a spectacular occasion. I stood outside on the wide pavement, looking up at the great building. The audience waited patiently to enter the Opera House. The men were mostly dressed in formal black evening suits, military uniform or frock coats, and the ladies in long flowing gowns in varying shades of cream and white. Scattered among the opera patrons were the artisans, for whom such an experience was like a precious jewel, the men easily identified by their less formal dress of velvet jackets, knee-breeches and flowing neckties. Inside there was an atmosphere of expectancy and I couldn't help gasping as my eyes caught sight of the staircase rising from the foyer to the Grand Circle. We ascended the staircase as it curved to the right, passing the gallery of paintings and moving through the expertly carved arches and statues, standing as if protecting the unique architecture.

We had excellent seats. I stole a glance upwards to the five tiers of seats around the auditorium, and was struck by the large number of people standing at the rear of the upper levels. At the end of the evening, as I thanked my host, I admitted that I was unsure whether the quality of the music or the experience of the building had had the greatest impact on me.

The next evening I was in for yet another Viennese experience. I was going to the Burgtheater to see *The Fugitive* and in the company of the author himself. Again it was difficult to choose between the quality of the acting and the stunning environment of the early Baroque-style theater. I was overwhelmed as we ascended the grand staircase with the sculptured balustrades. However, what I was unprepared for were the ceiling paintings by the young master Gustav Klimt, one of which depicted Shakespeare's theater at Stratford-upon-Avon, less than twenty miles from my home. During the performance I couldn't help but gaze at the four-tiered auditorium with the central chandelier hovering over yet another elegant audience. The ladies and gentlemen of Vienna certainly knew how to dress for an occasion.

Herzl didn't sit with us but greeted us after the performance which had been politely, if not enthusiastically, applauded by the audience. "We'll take some supper at the Imperial Hotel, which is within walking distance," he said as he took his wife's arm and beckoned me to follow as we strolled along the Burgring.

We entered yet another impressive Viennese building as we witnessed guests arriving and departing. Herzl gestured for us to wait in the lounge whilst he arranged a table for supper. Julie Herzl and I took a couple of seats in the lounge, surrounded by mirrors reaching up to the first-floor level. The room was dominated by chandeliers but was rather dark due to the large number of drapes, marble walls and alcoves. We weren't kept waiting long as Herzl beckoned us to enter the restaurant through a smallish door on the right of the reception.

I realized that as delightful as all this was, the main purpose of my visit was to engage with Herzl. We all had a most enjoyable supper and when it seemed a convenient time I politely excused myself, bowed gently to Julie, and shook hands with her husband, before leaving the elegant Imperial Hotel. I walked slowly along the Burgring and contemplated my next meeting with Herzl.

CHAPTER THREE

Paris, France, 1891–1894

It was Wednesday October 13, 1891, and I was arriving in Paris at the Gare du Nord. It was the day after the most solemn day in the Jewish calendar, the Day of Atonement, Yom Kippur. I'd been surprised to see flurries of snow out of the train window and had been assured by a fellow passenger that this was an unusually early fall. The purpose of my journey was to again meet with Herzl, who'd been appointed at the early age of thirty, by the Viennese newspaper *Neue Freie Presse* as its Paris correspondent.

I was eager to meet him again, to reignite the spark of excitement I'd first observed in him when we'd met in Vienna barely a year earlier. I knew my visit was a gamble; Herzl had been in Paris for just a few days, and although I'd written to say I was planning to visit him, my letter had gone unanswered. I wondered if my impetuous trip would be premature, if he was too busy settling into his new home and employment – or if indeed he even remembered me.

I emerged from the station, holding my valise, reflecting on the sheer elegance which was the hallmark of all the Parisian railway stations. It was an impressive experience and the station was far more than just a destination. There was hustle and bustle, and even the restaurant boasted a menu of the highest quality and imagination. Standing outside for a few moments, I couldn't help but gaze up at the majesty of the structure designed by Hittorff, the architect who had also given Paris the Place de la Concorde and the Place de l'Etoile. Sitting atop the Gare du Nord were nine female figures, set against the Parisian skyline, looking down upon the square and the people, as if they were reflecting upon the influence of women on this city.

Had it not been for the continuous light snowfall and the state of the footway, I would have walked to the Hotel de Hollande in the Rue de la Paix, where Herzl was living and where I hoped to meet with him. Instead, I climbed aboard one of the horse-drawn cabs – fiacres – waiting in an orderly queue outside the station. The coachman glared at me from under his rather wet black beret as he sat hunched in the driver's seat – as if I'd interrupted his quiet snooze – and raised his bushy eyebrows as a substitute for asking my destination. I told him the Hotel de Hollande, climbed up the three steps and was jolted into my seat as the cab moved off. The horse, despite the blanket which had been covering its back, seemed rather happier than its owner to see me, and seizing the opportunity to warm itself, moved off, first at a slow step before breaking into a gentle trot.

It was not a long journey, but it was an inspiring one. The clip-clop of the horse's hooves and the rumbling wheels of the cab were muffled by the snow and created a kind of eerie atmosphere. I could see the evidence that remained from the Great International Exhibition of two years earlier, just 100 years after the start of the French Revolution. Rising over 200 meters to dominate the skyline was the tower built by Monsieur Eiffel to commemorate the event. You could smell the atmosphere of this grand European capital, Paris, beautiful in the rain, more so in the sunshine, but always beautiful; it breathed a culture so different from anything else I had experienced. I couldn't help but think I was in the middle of one of the most memorable periods of artistic innovation and imagination – a cultural revolution. This was a time in history when artists and composers, authors and poets, would create a legacy which would outlive them and inspire the generations that followed.

One of the features of the great railway stations of Paris is the way they connect to and through the main thoroughfares. We drove down Rue La Fayette, passing the junction with Boulevard de Magenta, and approached the Place de l'Opera, dominated by the splendor of the Opera House which had inspired *The Phantom of the Opera*. As we passed by, I gazed at the large posters advertising the opening performances of a Mahler symphony and promised myself that I mustn't leave Paris without a visit.

Leaving the Place de l'Opera we continued down the Rue de la Paix with barely a glimpse of the new department store Le Printemps. This is where I thought about England and my home town, Birmingham. Le Printemps was located on Boulevard Haussmann, named after Baron Georges-Eugène Haussmann, who was one of the driving forces in the development of modern Paris. It was Joseph Chamberlain, the mayor of Birmingham in the mid-1880s, 100 years before I assumed the same office, who'd been the great visionary force behind the redevelopment of that city and who'd wanted to replicate in Birmingham the boulevards and department stores of Paris.

I alighted from the cab outside the Hotel de Hollande. Once inside I looked for the reception desk and enquired if Dr. Herzl was available. With an exaggerated sweep of a hand, the elegantly dressed reception manager asked me to take a seat in the lounge. I picked up a copy of *Le Figaro* and began to try to read the news with my very limited knowledge of French. Combining the pictures with the words I understood, I could just about make out that there were widespread strikes in Paris and, across the border, severe industrial unrest in Berlin. Although I thought the flu outbreak had finished some months earlier, there were still reports of deaths from the epidemic which had already cost 6,000 lives.

I glanced up from the newspaper as a uniformed member of staff approached.

"Dr. Herzl is expected back shortly. Monsieur, would you care to wait?" I nodded in response, to which he asked me if I would take a cup of coffee or chocolate. "Indeed I would. Coffee, please," I replied.

I didn't have to wait long before a silver tray was brought bearing a china pot of coffee and a milk jug, together with a small croissant. At the same time I recognized the figure of Theodor Herzl entering the foyer. He was just as imposing as I remembered him in Vienna – black beard, good head of hair, holding his black silk hat and carrying several newspapers.

As he looked in my direction I stood up and advanced towards him. "Good afternoon, Dr. Herzl," I ventured. He paused with a mixture of recognition and vagueness which I wished to clarify without delay. "Bernard Zissman from England; I wrote to you a short while ago."

At this introduction, he smiled and offered his hand, which I grasped with enthusiasm. "Of course, welcome to Paris. How are you, my friend?" I was relieved that he had remembered our earlier meetings.

"I have an apology. I did receive your letter and I regret that my reply was somewhat late. By your presence it's clear you didn't receive it," he continued, "because I have to leave tonight for Vienna. My daughter Pauline is unwell and I must make arrangements for my wife Julie and the children to join me here in Paris."

I was obviously disappointed but the urge to hear more of Herzl's vision and what might motivate him in the future forced me to accept the news, if not with pleasure.

"I'll be away just for a few days. On my return we'll meet again, you'll spend some time with me and we'll explore this great city together, visit the theater, explore the galleries and speak of the changing face and influences of Europe."

It was the final words of his sentence which excited me the most. "I'll look forward to that. I'm sorry to hear the news of your daughter and I wish her well. I'll spend a day or two in Paris and return in a few weeks. As you'll recall, I'm fascinated by your own life and those influences upon it. I wish to discuss with you the changing face of Europe and how our people will benefit or not from those changes."

"We'll do that, Zissman, without fail. Sadly I have to admit to you that anti-Semitism is as rife here in Paris as back home in Vienna. It is one of the real diseases in our society. Of one thing I am sure, it will end in disaster and I wouldn't be surprised if also in conflict."

I couldn't be more astonished by his intuition, because the horrific consequences of what he was speaking about couldn't possibly have been foreseen. He glanced at the large grandfather clock which dominated the room, and then pleasantly surprised me by saying that he had a short time, as he put it, "to speak of England and Europe as we experience one of the great periods of cultural renaissance." As I drank my coffee, he spoke. "In Vienna, we've had some real delights. Richard Strauss recently completed his symphonic poem *Death or Transfiguration*, and Gustav Mahler has given us his First Symphony and, as if that was not enough, that great composer Rimsky-Korsakov's Symphonic Suite took St. Petersburg by storm."

I took this as a challenge and hoped that my memory would serve me well. "London has also had some significant events: Queen Victoria herself summoned Mr. D'Oyly Carte's opera company from the Savoy Theater to Windsor Castle to perform *The Gondoliers* and Her Majesty has shown her considerable delight to Mr. W.S. Gilbert and Sir Arthur Sullivan."

Herzl seemed to enjoy the exchange and continued. "I must tell you that here in Paris the locals are reading Emile Zola's *La Terre*, an unkind study of the peasant, and Victor Hugo's memorable story *Les Miserables*." I was sure he'd understand if I were to say that theater audiences throughout the world were being thrilled years later by the power of Claude-Michel Schönberg and Alain Boublil, who had moved to Paris at an early age, and whose musical stage experience re-created that great story of the French Revolution.

"But it is artists who are creating the Parisian excitement. They've finished mourning the passing of the Dutch painter Van Gogh and have become entranced by the talents of Toulouse-Lautrec," and with a twinkle in his eye, added, "whose delights are not just confined to his canvases."

He suddenly rose and, as he extended his hand as an indication that our meeting was at an end, said, "I must now excuse myself. When we next meet we'll resume the discussion about the future of the Jewish people, for I suspect that's the main object of your visit."

He didn't excuse himself before he enquired where I might stay in Paris. I assured him that my comforts were taken care of and that I'd write again to inquire about a more convenient time for us to meet.

We parted with warm and polite words. He continued to his room, while I went off towards the Rue de la Paix, where I was pleased to see the snow had stopped falling.

*   *   *

When I returned to Birmingham, I found a neatly handwritten letter, signed Dr. Theodor Herzl and dated Paris, October 4, 1891. It suggested that I delay my visit for about four to six months, when at which time he'd make me most welcome.

It was to be a few years before I made fresh arrangements. I wrote to Herzl to confirm my new arrival date and traveled by the same route, arriving in Paris on Thursday, October 18, 1894. I went straight to the Herzl home in Rue Monceau and found a warm welcome from Julie, who invited me into the house and showed me into a cozy lounge which was dominated, as in Vienna, by a desk with piles of newspapers and transcripts.

"Mr. Zissman, can I invite you take a cup of coffee, French coffee, unless you'd prefer a glass of schnapps? When Theodor returns from the office we'll have some supper." The generosity of her hospitality hadn't changed.

"A cup of coffee would be most acceptable," I replied, as she disappeared to a room at the rear of the house.

She reappeared instantly and I assumed that a maid would be bringing the refreshment. "I trust you had a pleasant journey from England. It's some time since I was last there. I do so enjoy the atmosphere and the shopping of London," said Julie with a glint in her eye, which showed the pleasure she felt from such visits. There was a pause and I detected an atmosphere in the room which I was unable to understand. Julie looked out of the window before quietly speaking.

"I hope you're not kept waiting long," she said as if in apology, "but my husband does not always hasten home. He works hard at the office with a very demanding editor in Vienna and, together with his own writing, he's often late and sometimes fails to come home at all."

To me, a comparative stranger, this seemed rather more than a courteous apology and I wondered if their relationship was strained. Before I could answer, I heard the banging of the front door and, to my surprise, and possibly his wife's too, Herzl strode into the room, a stern look on his bearded face, his hand reaching out to grasp mine. "My friend, it's good to see you again. There's so much to talk about in this ever-changing world of ours. Please forgive me if I've kept you waiting." With those words he threw several newspapers on to the table.

His entrance into the room was followed by a neatly dressed maid with a tray of coffee, some cake and two glasses, as if anticipating the arrival of her employer. After she departed I quickly assured him that I'd arrived only a short time earlier and that his wife had made me more than welcome. There was a fire burning in the grate, not all of the smoke disappearing up the chimney. Julie poured two cups of coffee and, opening a cupboard at the side of the mantelpiece, removed a bottle of cognac and poured a liberal measure for her husband.

"You can see that I quickly succumbed to the French custom of taking a glass of brandy on my return home," he said with a smile. "But I don't think your journey to Paris is to study my drinking habits," he added, and as I nodded, he continued. "Let's relax and talk about what's happening in Europe and what might happen in the coming months."

I spoke quickly before the conversation could get under way. "Before we begin, let me congratulate you on the birth of Trude [Margarethe] and, tell me, how is Pauline?" Both the Herzls reacted with what appeared to me a mixture of happiness and a little sadness, before Julie answered. "Thank you for asking. Trude is fine, a real Parisian. Pauline is not terribly well, but hopefully, now that the family is together, she'll improve." That appeared to be a signal to end the topic. Julie excused herself, presumably to supervise the preparation of the supper, and Herzl and I were left to carry on our conversation.

"How long have you now been in Paris?"

"I came here three years ago. You'll recall it was October 1891, initially for a four-month trial with the *Neue Freie Presse*. I wasn't able to give you any time then and I'm sorry that you had a wasted journey."

"Don't worry, I'm here now. So, my friend, how does life in Paris suit you?"

"Very well," came the reply. with what might have been a smile, barely recognizable behind the beard. "I'm not sure whether or not I like Paris; it's certainly different from Vienna. It's cosmopolitan, gay and, how can I describe it…" he paused, "it's somehow beautiful, genteel, even chic, and very inviting. Vienna was for me never quite like that." He paused again. "But you've arrived here at a particularly convenient time. I've just completed my new play."

"What's it called?" I asked, "and what, may I ask, is it about?"

"It's called *Das Neue Ghetto*, and what's most surprising is that it took me just nineteen days to write it."

I looked at him with surprise. "Well, it's either very short or you sat up throughout the night with a pen in your hand!"

"I have to say, it was a fierce challenge when I consider I wrote it simultaneously with all the other assignments expected of me, but then I'm well experienced in meeting a demanding timetable. There's an important point I must share with you, however," his voice dropped as if we were being observed, "the play will not bear my name as the author. I've agreed that it will appear under a pseudonym, 'Albert Schnabel', after a friend of mine. This is not to be shared with anyone, not even my family. So, my friend, I require from you too, a pledge that you will keep my secret safe."

I could think of no reason why I should divulge the secret, even if I was unaware of why Herzl had chosen this course of action. He sensed the question on my lips. "I don't wish to be known as an author, well, certainly not for some time, so that's the reason for the charade." He paused. "The play is in four acts written for fourteen parts, some of which are quite minor – like the domestic staff. The principal characters are Jews, some rather more assimilated than others, and the scene is set in Vienna. It's about Jewish society, the 'ghetto' complex, and something from which I ached to escape."

I began, for the first time, to understand this complicated man; his relatively non-religious background, his confrontation with anti-Semitism, and wondered for the first time if actually he wanted to escape from being a Jew. Clearly his views about his hometown of Vienna were not over-generous. He saw it as a city of culture and education but, I sensed, also a city of cold people and the very seat of anti-Semitism which had spread across the whole of Europe – even to those (few) countries where it hadn't previously existed.

"Jews here in France seem to want to be more like gentiles than the gentiles do themselves. They even dress their infants in white and take them to the synagogues to be received into Judaism, just like the Catholic children are dressed and received into the First Communion. Some rabbis adopt a similar dress to the Catholic priests, and you'll be surprised to learn that there was a proposal to hold Sabbath services on a Sunday. This seems to be assimilation at its worst, and I say that as one who believes in our people blending into the local population."

I found all of this interesting particularly as I had the benefit of some hindsight and knowing what Herzl would, within a few years, seek to propose for the Jewish people. Suddenly he rose and went and stood by the fireplace, head bowed, staring into the fire. He spoke softly, somehow out of character, as he pointed to the copy of *Le Figaro* which lay on the table.

"This has been a bad week for France and the Jews, and possibly the whole of Europe." He paused as he picked up a copy of a newspaper, not *Le Figaro* but another, which I could just see was called *La Libre Parole,* and I sensed he didn't expect a reply. "Just read this. On Monday a Jewish artillery officer, as yet unnamed, was arrested on charges of espionage. The talk in the cafés is that it is a man named Alfred Dreyfus, who is completely innocent of the charges. He does, of course, have connections with Germany, to whom he is alleged to have sold French military secrets, but I cannot help but speculate that it's his Jewish heritage which appears to be the reason for the charges. I'm worried, *very* worried about the implications of his arrest, and can only hope that in time, hopefully a short time, evidence will be produced to prove his innocence."

"What will be the next step?" I asked.

"Presumably a trial of some sorts, more likely a court-martial as he's in the army. I don't know when, but I hope that sufficient time is allowed for a defense to be prepared, as people already talk of 'flimsy evidence'."

At this point we were summoned into dinner, which was an elegant affair. We sat down around 8:30 and I wondered if the borscht followed by beef ragout and a very acceptable French red wine was being served for my benefit or if it was a typical Herzl menu. Conversation over the table continued as we discussed the comings and goings across Europe, and life in the great cities of London, Vienna and St. Petersburg.

"Tell us what is happening in London. My wife never seems to lose interest in stories of the great department stores, what is on the stage and news of the Royal Family." I wasn't sure if this was intended as a genuine request for news or an indication of Julie Herzl's interests, but I was happy to oblige.

"You'll probably have read in your newspapers and seen pictures in the magazines of the wedding last year of Queen Victoria's grandson, H.R.H. the Duke of York, and Princess Mary. It was indeed quite an occasion and, whilst it wasn't a public holiday, the whole country did celebrate, and Julie, you'd be interested to know that many went shopping or to the park." This brought a smile to the lips of my hostess and I couldn't help but speculate how royal weddings, seventy years later, would be seen on a screen in every home – not just in Britain, but worldwide.

"In March, didn't Mr. Gladstone finally give up office as prime minister?" Herzl interrupted with a rhetorical question. "Succeeded by Lord Rosebery, I believe, and didn't he marry Hannah Rothschild? What do you know of *his* reputation?"

"Yes that's so, but it's a little early to judge his reputation. We now have a new political party in England, the Labor Party, represented in the House of Commons by Mr. Keir Hardie, sent to Parliament by the voters of West Ham in London. As for Rosebery, he is of course a member of the House of Lords, well known throughout the Empire, and is a particular favorite of Queen Victoria, which Gladstone was not."

This seemed to end the conversation as I addressed Herzl's wife.

"May I say, Frau Herzl, that your beetroot borscht is probably the best I've ever tasted." I recalled that my mother used to serve it regularly at the festival dinner of Rosh Hashana and I could almost guarantee that if it were not me, then someone else at the table – in an attempt to cut into the potato, an essential ingredient in the soup – would splash their tie if they were lucky, or my mother's pristine tablecloth if they weren't.

The ragout was now being served in generous portions as the conversation moved across the Channel to Europe.

"It's interesting, what you say about Gladstone's Home Rule Bill, for in Russia, Czar Nicholas was having similar problems with his rule at home as he attempted to retain the old autocratic system, despite widespread opposition from the revolutionaries."

A stern look came across Herzl's face. "But I have to admit that it's the situation here in France that concerns me most. Two years ago a new newspaper was launched, *La Libre Parole*, in my view a dangerous journal, established to preserve and defend France against those who might destroy its Catholic base." He paused for a few moments and the opportunity was taken to pour some wine.

"Perhaps I should clarify that statement," he continued. "I'm not concerned that France should remain a Catholic country, in the same way that England might be regarded as a Christian country. It's good for a country to have a foundation of faith, whatever it may be, provided it's based on a tolerance of those whose religious faith is different from their own."

"And also, if I may interrupt you, provided that those who come to live in that country have an equal tolerance of the faith of their hosts and the generations who have striven to create and preserve it."

"Agreed," came the brief reply, "but here in France, as I've witnessed elsewhere, it's the dangerous words and actions of the few who strive to create fear and resentment by those who might somehow be different from them, have different beliefs and, at times, different interests and cultures. *La Parole* is preaching against the Freemasons, the republicans and, it won't surprise you, against the Jews too."

"Why is it," I asked, realizing the naivety of my question, "that throughout history our people have been so disliked, resented, and even feared? Surely, after all that the Jewish people have achieved and what so many individual Jews have given to the world, we should at last be accepted fully as equals, if not thanked."

"Therein lies the answer, my friend. We've given much in the fields of medicine and academia, in all the cultural disciplines, music, literature, the arts. And perhaps we've become arrogant with our own success, and this odd description emanating from the Bible of being the 'chosen people.'"

"So we're not just 'stiff-necked'?"

Herzl continued with just the hint of a smile at the mention of the biblical description of the obstinacy of the Hebrew people, as if I hadn't spoken. "The human being is a strange invention, whether created by the Almighty or by evolution. We understand the physical elements of man, his limbs and natural functions, we understand how he moves and how the bodily system works to recycle what he eats and drinks. We understand how, together with his female partner, he creates a succession so that when he dies his children continue the cycle of life. But what about the mind? I know Freud, not well I admit, and you recall we saw him in Vienna at the Sacher Hotel. He's attempted to explain the mind, but we're a long way from understanding it. There may be vast steps forward in the field of neurology which examines the brain, but as for the mind, well that's a different matter. Just think, and go back to the beginning of time. The Jews were the target of the Romans, the Greeks and the Persians. They were excluded from England in 1290, thrown out of Spain in 1492, indeed given barely four months to leave, and that was after a thousand years of dedicated and loyal service to Spain's economy and culture."

He began tutting and shaking his head as he continued, "There's anti-Semitism right across Europe: in Russia and in Poland, where it's worst of all, certainly in Austria where I've witnessed it personally. And now here in France, which is why I fear the accusation against Captain Dreyfus."

"This man Dreyfus, is he important – a key adviser to the government?"

"Not at all. Alfred Dreyfus is an unknown. He comes from Mulhouse in Alsace and his family, Jewish of course, moved to Paris around the time that Alsace was taken over by Germany, about twenty-three years ago after the Treaty of Versailles. We've not yet seen the full details of the accusation, but I'm hesitant to have any confidence in the French system of justice insofar as a Jew is concerned."

I was shocked by his statement, not just the words but the strength of feeling with which it was expressed.

I noticed that Julie Herzl was showing signs of fatigue, which I have to admit were reflected in my own feelings, and it seemed an appropriate time to excuse myself. Herzl was anxious that we meet up again and suggested that as the next day was Friday, he would take me on a tour of Paris when he finished work. I suppose I was mildly shocked by the suggestion, as the Sabbath eve was normally an occasion to be at home, but it was clear from his wife's reaction that this was one of his traditional activities on a Friday.

I was escorted to the door and with a slight bow to Julie and a handshake for Herzl, I offered my thanks, "You've both been most kind and your hospitality generous. I look forward to our meeting tomorrow," and turning to his wife. "I hope we'll meet again before I leave Paris."

"Indeed you will," he replied, "tomorrow", and with that, I left the Herzl home.

*   *   *

I was waiting in the lobby of my hotel when Herzl arrived to collect me. He was easily recognizable, square black beard with a traditional Viennese fur-collared coat and of course the silk top hat. I thought he was a little overdressed for a trip around the nightlife of Paris which, he hoped, would both excite and enlighten me.

Outside he had a cab waiting, and as we sat down, covering our legs against the chill of the autumnal evening, he instructed the driver to take us to a Montmartre café, the name given quickly in French, which escaped me. Once again I was treated to a journey through the cobbled streets of Paris, passing the elegant Le

Café Anglais. I decided to make the most of the "night on the town" as clearly my host planned to enjoy it too. It seemed that further conversation about the future of the Jewish people would have to be deferred to another time.

CHAPTER FOUR

Paris, France, 1896

On a cold day in January 1896, I was due to meet Herzl at the Café de la Paix overlooking the Place de l'Opera in Paris. I was on my way from Birmingham to Berlin, while he was in Paris for a brief interview for *Neue Freie Presse* of which he was now the editor. When I arrived he was sitting with a cup of coffee, talking to a youngish woman with two children. On the table was an open newspaper covering a bundle of others. As I approached, Herzl rose to his feet to grasp my hand warmly. The woman and children seemed somehow in another world, merely staring ahead.

"Zissman, it's good to see you again. I trust you're well." I nodded, and before I could utter a reply, he continued, "May I introduce Madame Lucie Dreyfus," and glancing at the children, "this is Pierre and – the pretty little girl." I bowed slightly to Madame Dreyfus and suspected that Herzl couldn't remember the little girl's name. The woman was, I guessed, around thirty years old but looked older. Her face appeared strained, her eyes slightly puffy and red, probably from crying, and certainly in need of sleep. Both children seemed a little nervous as they looked first at me, then at Herzl, and finally at their mother, who had placed her arms around their shoulders as if the need to protect them was uppermost in her mind.

It didn't take a genius to know that this was the wife and children of Captain Alfred Dreyfus, now sitting in prison on Devil's Island some thousands of miles away off the coast of French Guinea in West Africa.

My thoughts were interrupted by the arrival of a waiter, thin and looking rather bad tempered, wearing a white shirt and matching apron tied around his black trousers. His appearance and demeanor indicated that his shift might just be coming to an end.

Herzl looked at Mme. Dreyfus and then at me, "Tea or coffee?"

"Tea, please; nothing for the children."

"Coffee for me, please." The order was given to the waiter, including a portion of cake for the children. Herzl spread out in front of us the newspaper he'd been reading, *Le Siècle*. "Here on the front page is the list of charges against your husband. It's the first time they've been published and we can be grateful to Monsieur Yves-Guyot, who has displayed the courage, indeed the integrity, to print them." A brief sob came from Madame Dreyfus, and it was obvious how much strain she'd been living under since her husband had been convicted a year earlier, in December 1894. I couldn't help but wonder if the stories circulating around the city about her husband's infidelity were known to her and how much impact this would have had on her. But adultery was not a crime, neither in the nineteenth century, nor in the centuries that followed.

"It is nothing short of a disgrace on France, the French army and all who claim to believe in *Liberté, Egalité, Fraternité*, that such trumped-up and flimsy charges could be brought and never challenged by those in authority." With these words he thumped the table, frightening the children, who clung closer to their mother, startling others in the café seeking quiet relaxation over a cup of coffee or glass of cognac.

Lucie Dreyfus placed a hand on his arm as if to calm him, as gradually everyone else around us returned to their own conversations.

"Thank goodness there are men of Yves-Guyot's caliber, ready to stand up for justice and fight for Dreyfus's freedom, because it's long been denied by the rotten disease of anti-Semitism which currently seems to flow through the blood of the French."

"I thought that fresh evidence had been uncovered some two years ago," I ventured. "Why hasn't this been used to convict the true culprit?"

"Because, my friend, the army has closed its ranks, like all armies, but on this occasion, to defend the wrong person. The Head of Military Intelligence, I believe his name was Henri Piquart, holding the rank of lieutenant-colonel, had discovered that the real traitor was a Major Esterhazy, but no action was taken."

"Why not?"

"Because if there is one characteristic of armies throughout history and the world, it is that after defending their countries, they defend themselves."

Lucie Dreyfus rose from the table and, taking the hands of her children, she turned to Herzl with a smile and tears in her eyes. "Thank you so much for your company, Monsieur Herzl, and for the tea and cake for the children. I hope we'll meet again soon." Her voice dropped until it was scarcely audible. "And thank you for your support and loyalty during this terrible time in our lives." With these words she quickly walked away, as if to return to her own world. We both sat for a few moments, without speaking, as we gazed after the three of them. "That was a terrible day; the date is etched forever in my mind: Saturday January 5, 1895. One of the reasons I recall it so clearly was because it was so cold. Even though it was winter, it was particularly cold, and I'd worn my heaviest coat. It had rained throughout most of the night and we'd stood for some time to witness what was to be the final degradation of Captain Dreyfus."

He continued. "I was one of the fortunate ones. The journalists had joined the diplomats and other dignitaries – indeed I could see Sarah Bernhardt, in a special section – whilst the public were kept outside the gates of the Ecole Militaire courtyard in the Place de Fontenoy."

Herzl paused, as if recalling with pain those final minutes of the act which saw Dreyfus stripped of his gold braid and his brightly polished buttons torn from his military uniform.

"That day will live in my memory until I die. Dreyfus's dignity and bearing reflecting his continued claim of innocence as he marched with his head held high, even though the anti-Semitic newspapers had tried to caricature him as a sniveling Jewish traitor being dragged with his head bowed to his rightful punishment. It was of course the Sabbath, the ceremony having been postponed from the previous day, so there were few Jews present."

"Was there no one prepared to defend him on that day?" I inquired, without expecting a reassuring reply.

"Strange as it seemed, the commandant, Ferdinand Forzinetti, didn't believe Dreyfus to be guilty, but was unable to intervene. As the ceremony proceeded I could hear the crowds shouting with enthusiasm 'Death to the Jews', drowning out the dignified and repeated words of Dreyfus as he proclaimed *'Vive La France.'*"

There was another pause as Herzl seemed to recall the pictures of that day in his memory as he continued in a barely audible tone, "And then, strangely, the muted sobs of those who still believed in French justice were silent as were the shouts of the crowd. All that could be heard was a loud crack, as Dreyfus's sword was snapped across the raised knee of the officiating officer of the Republican Guard, the final degradation of an officer and the destruction of a fine man."

It seemed to me not the time to interrupt his recollection of this event, which clearly was to have such a dramatic impact on Herzl and, with the benefit of hindsight, upon the Jewish people and so many others too. We rose from the table and started to stroll away from the Café de la Paix and down the Rue de la Paix.

"I expect this event was to change you and some of your ambitions?" I asked.

"Well, yes, it had an influence on me, a very big influence. But you know, my friend, it only confirmed views I'd held for many years."

I looked at him with growing interest and an air of anticipation. "I'd been thinking for some years that anti-Semitism was, how might you say, like a killer disease in the human mind," he said.

"Throughout my university days in Vienna, when I was excluded from circles in which I wished to mix, suspicion of the Jew was ever-present, like a lingering cloud threatening rain at any time and which would break out into either continuous drizzle or a violent thunderstorm." His voice rose as he gave vent to his feelings. "And now this terrible act of anti-Semitism, here in the country which supposedly gave birth to the principle of liberty, confirms all that I've come to believe."

He stopped and turned to face me. "Zissman, our people, the Jewish people will never be free, never have the opportunity to be themselves, practice their religion and culture, and hold their heads as high as any other nation, *without a land of their own.*"

And so Herzl's mind was made up. A Jew, almost totally assimilated, but critical of assimilation itself, was about to publish *Der Judenstaat,* which was to plant the seeds of a movement that would change the direction of not just the Jewish people, but the whole of the Middle East and the entire world beyond.

It was perhaps a moment in history to cherish and remember. Herzl's life was about to take a new turn, and the rest of us would be turning with him.

CHAPTER FIVE

London, England, 1896

I had received another brief handwritten note from Herzl to say that he would be in London in July and suggested a meeting at the Savoy Hotel in the Strand. At the time I didn't know he'd attended a mass meeting of East End London Jews the previous evening, when he told of his experiences which led to his dream of a Jewish National Home. I had arrived in good time. I certainly didn't wish to keep Dr. Herzl waiting. A secondary motive for my early arrival was that I'd never before been in the Savoy Hotel.

The hotel had opened seven years previously and it was clear from the décor that celebrations were to take place within the coming week. I couldn't help but notice two men walking through the lounge discussing the discreet work underway and whispers from an adjoining table suggested that one of them was Richard D'Oyly Carte, whose adjoining Savoy Theater had inspired him to build the hotel. He was accompanied by an immaculately dressed man, whose demeanor and authority indicated that he was obviously the French manager, César Ritz, who'd been lured with his team from Paris to manage the Savoy's reputation for impeccable service and attention to detail. A waiter, dressed in black tailcoat and trousers, white shirt and bow tie, both starched to perfection, discreetly arrived at my table and asked if he could be of service. I'd taken the opportunity to glance around the lounge and I ordered some coffee and cake, which appeared to be what the other guests were enjoying.

I'd taken a seat that would give me a good view of the entrance to the lounge and I was fascinated by those who entered. There was a sudden murmur which spread throughout the hotel, starting in the foyer, as a group entered and everyone's attention was drawn as Ritz led the group to a quiet corner of the lounge. It was none other than the Prince of Wales, later to become King Edward vii, out with friends in London for some leisurely entertainment. As they passed by, the occupants of each table rose and bowed respectfully. Whilst his friends took their seats, the Prince wandered over to another table occupied by two ladies, and greeted both with a kiss on the hand. It was clear that his attention was directed to the taller of the two who was, without a doubt, both beautiful and elegant. I suspected from stories I'd read that this was no other than Mrs. Lillie Langtry, the socialite, who'd shocked society by becoming a stage actress.

I wasn't kept waiting long. At precisely four o'clock, the time we'd agreed to meet, my observation of London's top society was interrupted and I saw Herzl standing at the doorway, looking around. His distinguished figure, striking black beard and hair, immaculately dressed in black frock coat and holding his tall black silk top hat, somehow commanded the attention of the other guests. I stood proudly and raised a hand, as if to shout, "He's here to meet me." Herzl nodded and made his way to my table. We shook hands and after a brief and courteous exchange of words, I invited him to sit and inquired if he'd take some tea or coffee or whether he'd prefer something stronger.

"I'll have coffee, if I may, but nothing to eat." He paused before continuing, a glint of excitement in his eye, and a lilt in his voice. "I've had some wonderful news which I simply cannot keep to myself."

It seemed inappropriate, if not rude, to interrupt his flow.

"Next week I'm due to meet with Baron Edmond de Rothschild at his Paris office." This was of course the leading member of the Rothschild family, the great and respected banking dynasty.

"It's been an exhilarating year for me, very tiring with much traveling, and last night I was engaged in a unique experience right here in London." He didn't wait for my question before continuing his explanation. "I'm not sure if I told you that I'd been received in your fine Houses of Parliament by Sir Samuel Montagu, an experience which was both grandiose and inspiring. One of my initial thoughts was how this visit makes Britain great, the opportunity for the ordinary citizen to enter into its seat of government without challenge."

I couldn't help but think how, a century later, those very same Houses of Parliament would be protected by a ring of concrete and armed policemen, such a contrast to the welcome received by Dr Herzl.

"Montagu seemed to me a very good Jew and was encouraging. He pledged his support for our movement but only if three critical conditions could be met. He introduced me to Asher Myers of the *Jewish Chronicle* and Reverend Singer, who I believe has recently translated the *Daily Prayer Book* for the Hebrew Congregations of the British Empire."

I found it hard to believe that this was the very same daily prayer book still in use by Orthodox synagogues throughout the western world. "These conditions – were they achievable?" I inquired.

A stern look came over his face. "They were huge obstacles which I was unsure of my ability to overcome. He required that the hugely wealthy Hirsch Foundation must hand us millions of pounds from its coffers and Baron Edmond de Rothschild must join the committee. As if this isn't sufficient a challenge, I'm required to gain the support of the leaders of the Great European Powers who must agree to our plan."

This seemed a mighty set of conditions to me, almost as if Montagu wished him to fail, but I could see he wasn't totally dispirited. "So that's why I'm seeing the worthy Baron Rothschild next week, but I interrupt myself: I was about to relate the story of last evening's meeting. It was a mass meeting of shouting and excited East Enders, all young Zionists, and considering the terrible weather I was surprised and delighted by the numbers who attended. Would you believe that when I was introduced to speak, I was compared to Moses and even Columbus! I'm afraid I got carried away in my oratory and when I sat down – having urged the audience to fight for the establishment of a Zionist home which would be protected by a Jewish army – the crowd were on their feet roaring their approval." Herzl stopped, appearing exhausted from relating the story as if he'd just finished his actual speech.

"So how do you see the chances of success?" I asked. I was only too well aware of Herzl's commitment to the establishment of a Jewish National Home, preferably in Palestine, but having to consider alternative locations suggested by European leaders.

He lowered his head into his hands for just a moment or two before replying. "Success, what is that, my friend? I've been privileged to meet with the wealthy, the influential, those with power and those who seek it. I've left meetings as if walking high on a cloud, and then others as if in despair. I've been received into the courts and offices of those who rule and influence not just our continent, but the world. Here in London I must admit to being discouraged when I met with two gentlemen, Claude Montefiore and Frederick Mocatta, who flatly refused to commit the support of the Liberal Jewish Community. On the instigation of the great Israel Zangwill I attended the Maccabean Club on two occasions. The first was last year, I recall a foggy miserable day in London, with the atmosphere at the meeting equally cool when I shared my plans for the first time in public, and a second time, when the reception was distinctly warmer – and I have to admit the dinner rather better. I believe they approved of my speech, and without dissent, agreed to make me an honorary member. I felt deeply privileged. There were interesting reports in London's *Jewish Chronicle* and the editor, Asher Myers, whom I met at the

Maccabean dinner, wrote about my plans being the 'Solution to the Jewish Question.'"

The mention of Zangwill's name conjured up fresh excitement in my mind. One of the great characters of Jewish history and literature, his books – starting with *Children of the Ghetto* – had captured the atmosphere of Jewish life in London's East End as he described how Jews sought to reconcile their lives in the ghetto with their participation in a modern world. Zangwill was to become an outstanding advocate for Zionism, but I was always concerned about some of his views on the future of the Arab inhabitants of Palestine, who he would have preferred to see living in one of the neighboring countries.

Herzl didn't appear to notice my brief lapse in attention. "But there is better news. I was confused by the attitude of Colonel Albert Goldsmid, a British army officer, born I believe in Bombay and who, despite being the son of baptized Jews and growing up as a Christian, seems to have returned to his roots at an early age. Whilst he had expressed the strong view that Palestine was the only option for the Jewish National Home and had actually wanted to charter boats to help colonize Palestine, he seems to have become ambivalent about the whole idea more recently.

"In April on a warm spring day, I spent two and a half hours one afternoon in Karlsruhe with the Grand Duke Friedrich of Baden and I remain grateful to Reverend Hechler, who is the chaplain to your British Embassy in Vienna, for kindly arranging that appointment. I returned to my hotel, the Germaine, to take some Bavarian beer. I reflected on a magnificent meeting which followed a most comfortable journey in the elegant and memorable Orient Express. The Grand Duke was kind and warm, a man of simple nobility with a deep faith in natural justice, and he facilitated opportunities for me to meet many in the German ruling circle. I believe he took my idea seriously. Just a month later I was back in Vienna to be ushered into the presence of Papal Nuncio Agliardi, a tall slender man with thinning gray hair, who appeared to me to be set in his ways and well bred. Beyond all of that, we have been encouraged by the Zionists in Vienna and Sofia, as well as the hassidim in Poland. I have to tell you, Zissman, our mass movement is growing."

He'd been talking for some time and seemed to be tiring, so I suggested he drink another cup of coffee. I poured a cup from the shining silver pot, which boasted the discreet coat of arms of the Savoy Hotel. Herzl again declined an offering of some cake or a sandwich.

"I know that you've recently returned from Constantinople. How was that visit?" I inquired.

"I hope you've some time to listen, as that was an interesting and in many ways a fruitful meeting. I traveled to Constantinople just two or three weeks ago and stayed for about ten days between June 17 and 28. It wasn't my choice to stay for so long but my attempts to obtain an audience with Sultan Abdul Hamid were frustrated and I had to be satisfied with a series of meetings with his advisors and government officials. I'd arrived somewhat tired after a two-day journey through the night. I'd been introduced to Herr Philip Michael de Nevlinski last May and had been assured that he had excellent connections with the Constantinople establishment. I have to say, I'm not convinced that I can trust this man, he is after all a Polish autocrat and probably inclined to be an anti-Semite, but it was imperative that I use whatever connections I had, to meet with the Ottoman sultan."

"Tell me about Constantinople and the Ottomans." I couldn't possibly mention that the Ottoman Empire had crumbled, and the city was now called Istanbul.

"The Ottoman dynasty had a total commitment to preserve the three holy places, Medina, tomb of the Prophet Muhammad, Mecca, the focus of Islamic prayer, and Jerusalem from where Muhammad departed for heaven. Constantinople was the capital of both the Roman and Byzantine Empires and now the Ottoman Empire. It's a city I'm very fond of and I had several opportunities to see it as we traveled around from one audience to another. It has both beauty and ugliness; it has palatial as well as dilapidated buildings, there's much greenery within the city, and when the sun shines on the mass of glorious domes on the multitude of mosques, it's as if heaven is looking down upon the city. There's a sign of commercial activity resulting no doubt from the number of ships which sail up and down the Bosporus Strait."

His visits had clearly influenced Herzl's view of Constantinople as a city, although in later years his impressions of the city were destined to change. I decided to press him about the success of his mission and whether he felt as satisfied with the people of the city.

"I was welcomed by two Greek journalists and Baron Berthold Popper. This gave me encouragement as he was an Austrian Jew and a good friend of my father-in-law, Jacob Naschauer, which I thought would make for better understanding. Nevlinski and I stayed in a suite at the Royal Hotel and he arranged for a whole array of people to meet me, but not the sultan. I met with the grand vizier and, through my own initiative, also with his son. Nevlinski arranged for me to see the chief secretary of foreign affairs and eventually with the man most influential with the sultan, Izzet Bey. This meeting took place at Yildiz, the home of the Turkish government. I felt I was making slow but steady progress and then I was introduced to Daoud Effendi, an Ottoman Jew, who expressed to me the fears of the Jewish community about upsetting the good relations enjoyed with the sultan. I had in mind to bestow some fine gifts on Turkey in exchange for Palestine," Herzl paused as he saw my eyebrows rise in response to this statement, "but the sultan felt that by agreeing to such a proposal, however generous the gifts, he would upset the whole of Islam if he ever considered selling Palestine to the Zionists."

I had to admit that with the benefit of hindsight I understood the sultan's attitude. Herzl, however, was determined that he couldn't return from Constantinople empty-handed. If he wasn't able to say that progress had been made with some agreement from the Turks, then he felt that much would be lost. He was by no means a man who sought material recognition, but asked

Nevlinski to inquire if the sultan would bestow an honor on him so that he could return with some status to continue his efforts to convince the Turkish government of the Zionist case. This was agreed and, to Herzl's surprise, he was awarded the Commander's Cross of the Mejidiye Order, a practice Herzl later learned was the sultan's custom when he wished to influence visiting dignitaries. Along with the decoration came the request for a loan of two million francs, which was not surprising considering the current Ottoman debt of over one hundred million pounds sterling. It was this request that led to the meeting with Sir Samuel Montagu in the Houses of Parliament.

Satisfied with his trip to Constantinople, Herzl passed through Sofia, the Bulgarian capital, where hundreds of people awaited him on the railway station platform to welcome and applaud him, shouting, "Next Year in Jerusalem". Herzl observed that, "I have to tell you how moved I was when this wonderful friendly crowd escorted me to the local Zionist Society and synagogue where even more people were present."

As he continued his mission, Herzl was clearly beginning to feel that his vision had the chance of becoming a reality. These were impressive contacts and I was inquisitive as to how they came about and, more importantly, what they achieved. I realized from our conversations that what Herzl required more than anything else was the endorsement of Europe's leaders of what he was seeking to achieve, and a personal stamp on himself as the leader of the movement, so that the Jews themselves would also recognize his authority.

"I was never really comfortable with Hechler," he continued. "It was not just his eccentric appearance and long gray beard reminiscent of some biblical prophet, but I doubted his motives, which I suspected were more about an ambition to become Protestant Bishop of Jerusalem. But as he believed my objectives were biblically inspired, I felt it appropriate to use whatever avenues were open to me to secure the necessary meetings. The grand duke was concerned that if my mission succeeded, then too many Jews would emigrate from Germany, taking with them the capital which his country badly needed. He was also hesitant to support the Zionist movement, lest his motive might be misunderstood as a wish to get rid of the Jews. If I had a private view, and this is difficult to admit," he smiled as he related this piece of the story, "I doubt he regarded me capable of bringing about this great opportunity to meet the grand duke even though I had spent time on my dress and appearance for such a vital discussion. My meeting with the grand duke was indeed encouraging and I was confident he would discuss the ideas with his uncle, the kaiser. However, I felt little optimism following the meeting with Agliardi. I found him to be disinterested, even negative, and I don't think he perceived the establishment of a national home as the solution to the Jewish problem. But you should be comforted because I was fortunate in getting a copy of my book, *Der Judenstaat*, into the hands of Mr. Gladstone, courtesy of Sir Samuel Montagu, and I'm told he was impressed by what he read. Later this month I journey to Karlsbad to meet with Prince Ferdinand of Bulgaria, and if I'm fortunate I'll then return to Vienna for an audience with the Turkish ambassador, Mahmud Nedim Bey. But to me, there is a much greater target I need to reach, and that is the Ottoman sultan."

"What drives you on this mission? It's as if you bear on your shoulders the future of every Jew in the world."

He smiled, as if not fully recognizing the weight of responsibility I'd just attributed to him.

"Many people think that my desire to see the Jews restored to their natural homeland stemmed from my covering the Captain Dreyfus case. But my feelings were stirred even before this terrible case. I'd seen and witnessed in my student days in Vienna, even more so in Paris when I arrived there to report for the *Neue Freie Presse*, how the disease of anti-Semitism was endemic in non-Semitic peoples. The Jewish people are one people and however hard they've attempted to blend with the host nations who've offered them a home, they've never been able to shrug off their Jewishness or the culture which binds them together. That's why I describe them as *one people*."

I sensed he was about to share with me what lay behind the publication of *Der Judenstaat*, which had been released just a few months before our meeting here in London.

"Why do you feel that however hard we've tried to become loyal citizens, we still meet such suspicion and loathing?" I asked, without necessarily expecting an answer.

"What you ask is incapable of a logical answer. We've been loyal, excellent patriots, perhaps too loyal. Wherever we've lived, we've served our countries with distinction. We've enhanced the quality of life by our contribution to the arts, especially music, to science and to trade and the economic success of governments and I have to tell you, it's been *in vain* – and I suspect it will *always* be in vain." I listened with the benefit of hindsight to his brief and visionary foresight.

I pushed the cup of coffee towards him, as if to suggest that a break in his words might be appropriate, but he was in full flow and not yet ready to rest.

"Whichever land we've chosen to live in, and for however long – be it just a few years or centuries – we're still seen as aliens. But, and this is part of my inspiration which has never ceased to amaze me, we seem incapable of extermination, no matter how hard our enemies try. No people has suffered so much and for so long. Our people have been persecuted beyond the limits most can endure and we've remained strong and faithful to our heritage and our forefathers. And I say to you, assimilation is a simple and cruel remedy."

As he paused, I couldn't help but speculate how he reconciled this statement with his own life, which had come so close to full assimilation within the city of Vienna.

"There is but one piece of land which historically is the land of the Jewish people, and that is Palestine, the Promised Land."

"But is that not in the very heart of the world which poses the greatest threat to its existence?" I countered, knowing how the establishment of the tiny State of Israel had united every Arab nation both on Israel's borders and beyond in one single objective, to extinguish its life even on the day it breathed its first breath of freedom and independence.

Herzl looked at me as he stroked his beard. "You speak as so many Jews do, influenced by the culture and settled life of the European nations, but do not be misled. We are an economic convenience which quickly becomes a political inconvenience. We are a problem, a problem in France, a problem in Austria, in Germany and yes, here in England too. I wonder how long it might be before we become a problem in that bastion of freedom, the United States of America. We *can* live in peace with our neighbors and we have to *learn* how to achieve that. We can build together, with our neighbors, a region rich in culture and science, which will bring a quality of life to those who live there, and which will be the envy of the world."

His voice was rising and beginning to attract the attention of those guests who'd watched him enter the lounge. I hesitantly lifted a hand and once again pushed the cup of coffee towards him, offering him a slice of my cake.

Herzl smiled, realizing he was being overtaken by his own enthusiasm, refused the cake and lifted the elegant china cup to his lips.

"I suspect there's much work yet to do, despite the traveling and tremendous energy you've already expended on this mission," I said, "and forgive me if I interrupted you."

He brushed my apology aside. "There's so much to tell and it's difficult to know where to start. Of course I've been influenced by last year's totally unjust degradation of Captain Dreyfus and, not long after this event, the municipal election victories by anti-Semitic parties in Vienna. It was a year or two before that an insignificant event occurred, which only added to my conviction that the answer to what is known as the 'Jewish problem' is a Jewish National Home."

I was puzzled by this reference and asked him for an explanation, which he happily offered.

"It was the death in Paris of Captain Armand Mayer, who died in a duel resulting from a challenge about an anti-Semitic campaign in the French newspaper *La Libre Parole.*"

I began to understand how so many different factors had convinced Herzl about his mission in life. Anti-Semitism appeared to have been a part of his life from the time he was at university, through his time as journalist, to the time of our meeting. No single event had resulted in his belief.

"What I seek is not just the establishment of a Jewish home, but the restoration of a state. One would hope for a short journey to such an achievement, but I doubt that. It may well fall to the vision and determination of future generations of Jews to see my dream become a reality. *But, this I tell you, if you will it, it is no dream.* I am surrounded by Jews who possess the wealth and the influence to make it happen, but they are too content within the comfort of the societies in which they reside."

I sat mesmerized by this man's vision and the power of his language – and at the early age of just thirty-six. I spoke in words hardly louder than a whisper, "Are you saying that your efforts will merely be the start of the journey?"

"Indeed so, for it is the inauguration of such a venture which is the key to its ultimate success. It takes commitment and courage to start on the road to the establishment of a national state. It is rare in history that those who look into the future see the fruits of success. There are too many of our people who cry from the heart about the threat of anti-Semitism but who do nothing to offer a solution. I hold the conviction that without a national home we shall never see the end of anti-Semitism."

I looked at him with a sense of amazement which he wouldn't be able to comprehend. For this was the close of the nineteenth century, and it was to be barely forty years before the world would witness the horrors of one of the most barbaric times in Jewish history, as the Nazis marched across Europe.

We'd been sitting for some time and a waiter hovered courteously, if not expectantly, nearby. "May I offer you schnapps or another coffee?" I asked. "A glass of schnapps would be more than welcome," came the answer, and I turned to the waiter to order the glass together with a cup of chocolate for myself.

"So do you not think there are viable alternative locations for this national home," I inquired, "perhaps somewhere in Europe where so many of our people have lived for generations, or perhaps in the New World, the United States of America, where so many seek to live?"

"Not so, my friend. There have been suggestions, made to satisfy everyone but the Jewish people. There is one place on earth which is the historic and unforgettable homeland, and that is Palestine. It is in this land where the Jews will find peace and a new self-respect. This is the land where we'll once again end our wandering in the wilderness."

I didn't know how to react to this prediction. Herzl didn't have the advantage I had, of knowing what result a Jewish state would have on the Middle East. My mind filled with the pictures of the establishment of the new Jewish state just fifty or so years ahead. How I wanted to bring Herzl to see the reality of his dream. Peace had *not* been achieved, and perhaps it would take another man of Herzl's stature and vision to bring about all that he had striven for in his lifetime.

My meeting with Herzl was clearly drawing to a close, and as he was about to gather his belongings, we both noticed the entrance of a small group concentrating their attention on a well-dressed lady, wearing what appeared a typically Parisian hat. Herzl glanced in her direction and spoke quietly. "Ah, Madame Sarah Bernhardt, she stays here when she is playing on the London stage. She is precisely the kind of figure our movement needs at this time." Perhaps he thought I might not be fully aware that she was the eldest illegitimate daughter of a Dutch Jewish mother and, although baptized, never turned her back on her heritage.

Herzl drank his cognac with one or two gulps and rose to excuse himself. "Thank you for the hospitality, it's been a pleasure to talk with you, and after next week when I've met with Baron Rothschild perhaps there'll be good news to report." With these words he offered his hand, which I shook with vigor, picked up his hat and swept out of the lounge.

It was to be some months before we were to meet again, an occasion for which I couldn't wait.

CHAPTER SIX

Vienna, Austria, 1897

Summer in Vienna is a charming time and I was sitting in a well-worn chair in a first-floor office at number 9 Türkenstrasse. It was the office where Herzl was striving to publish his newspaper, *Die Welt*, and the floor was strewn with discarded pieces of paper, presumably draft articles which had been read, re-read and finally rejected. Herzl was sitting behind a low desk which, to my inexpert eye, appeared to be made of pine and which had been finished in a glossy black color. Behind the desk were a couple of large brown classical bookcases suffering from neglect and becoming distinctly discolored with time. What was surprising was that they appeared to be made of different woods – I wondered if this was the style of the time or to keep the cost down – and I noticed the contrasts of the pine, walnut and oak. They were complemented with a rather elegant set of brass door handles.

There was another guest in the room, a distinguished-looking man, in his late forties, with receding hair – which appeared to be turning white prematurely – and a magnificent matching beard and mustache. Herzl introduced him to me as Herr Max Nordau, an old and valued friend with similar aspirations for the Jewish people. Nordau, like Herzl, was from Pest, the son of a rabbi, and had been brought up Orthodox. It was surprising that he was now an atheist, but totally committed to the establishment of the Jewish National Home.

"Gentlemen, may I invite you take some tea, coffee, or even a glass of schnapps?" asked our host, in reply to which Nordau requested schnapps whilst I was happy to drink coffee. Herzl went to the door, opened it and quietly instructed whoever was in the adjacent room to bring the drinks and some biscuits.

I looked at both these men in whose presence I felt dwarfed, not just by their stature, but by the contribution they would both make to Jewish history. It was the eve of a meeting destined to change the world. We would travel to Basel in Switzerland the next day, where I would watch whilst the arrangements for the first Zionist Congress were finalized. Herzl had worked long and hard to achieve this gathering of Jewish leaders from around the world, who would meet with a small number of non-Jewish supporters to give birth to the dream to establish a national home for the Jewish people.

The door swung open and a young man pushed his way in, carrying a rather battered tray bearing the drinks and biscuits. He put the tray on a table and his stare gave away his view that there were more important tasks to perform than waiting at table. His trousers were somewhat baggy and his shirt was stained with what appeared to be printer's ink. He left the room with a polite acknowledgment from Herzl.

Nordau spoke first, having sipped at his glass of schnapps. "Herzl, how many do you expect at Basel?"

"I imagine more than 100, but less than 300," came the reply in a disappointing tone. "I'd hoped for more, but those who *do* attend will take their place in history."

"What about the great families of Judaism – the Rothschilds, Montefiores?" Before he could continue, Herzl interrupted sharply.

"My friends, not only will the Rothschilds and Hirsches as well as other financial leaders of our people not be present, but I've asked that they are not referred to in any speech which is delivered. I'm disappointed with both the barons, particularly Hirsch, for although he died three months ago on one of his estates in Hungary, he'd been most generous to our people. He became committed to the resettlement of the Russian Jews but directed them to Argentina. I believed that to be a flawed policy for it was based entirely on philanthropic objectives rather than creating a national Jewish State."

Nordau raised his hand, "Baron Hirsch enjoyed an outstanding reputation, he created a personal fortune of some $100 million by 1890, and much of this resulted from his interests in railways and the sugar and copper industries. Don't you think you should have reflected more wisely on his ideas as well as your own?"

"Maybe, but as I think he regarded my vision as pure fantasy, so it seemed futile to pursue the Baron further," said Herzl, "but I admit that the concession he gained enabling him to control the Turkish railways with considerable success did no harm to my approaches to the government in Constantinople."

I'd heard about the reputation of Baron Hirsch. He had given the Alliance Israelite Universelle one million francs to create schools, and later established a foundation which contributed 400,000 francs per annum to support education. Sadly, his only son had died in 1887. He was alleged to have said to a friend, "My son I have lost, but not my heir. Humanity is my heir."

Herzl rose from his chair as if about to make a dramatic statement. "I'm confident that we'll have a goodly number of representatives of our people, and what's more, I'll be disappointed if the world's press isn't present to witness this giant step forward in Jewish history." I wondered if we were to be told about Herzl's meeting with Rothschild, when he continued speaking. "As for Edmond de Rothschild, that was a fateful meeting. I had arranged to meet with him at his Paris office in Rue Lafitte on July 18 last year, and I have to tell you, it wasn't easy to arrange. It was imperative that I raised the loan of two million pounds demanded by the sultan of Turkey as a token of my authority and I'd been optimistic that this visit might produce success. When I arrived I found that Rothschild had invited Rabbi Zadoc Kahn, chief rabbi of Paris, and a Mr. Leven, the president of the Alliance Israelite, to be present, presumably to witness my request to him. I was comforted to some extent because I believed the chief rabbi to be an ardent Zionist and later he did write to me suggesting a secret conference of supporters so as not to alienate Rothschild, but this didn't find favor with me. So they tried hard to discourage me, citing the dangers my idea would pose for the Jewish people."

Turning to Nordau, Herzl continued, "and Max, do you know the result of that meeting? Mr. Leven advised the Turkish government that the Alliance Israelite would have nothing to do with our objective and had even forbidden its employees to join any Zionist body – indeed they were actively to oppose it."

This statement caused a silence to descend onto the room as we all began to absorb the strength of feeling and lengths to which those in such powerful positions would oppose Herzl's dream.

"It is equally discouraging when I hear that the chief rabbis of London and Vienna, Dr. Adler and Moritz Güdemann, have attacked us. and across the Atlantic, the Central Conference of American Rabbis have also expressed their disapproval. Where, I pray, is their belief in the divine future of the Jewish people?"

Nordau stroked his beard as he spoke quietly but with authority. "My dear Herzl, we shall not be diverted from our mission, we have the support of many governments and the sultan himself, and even more important, we have the strength of the Jewish people, so many of whom are suffering persecution; also the energetic support of young students across Europe, especially in Germany and Russia. It is for their future and the future of their children and grandchildren that we cannot now give up on our historic cause to establish a Jewish Home in Palestine. That is why our deliberations in Basel are so crucial. And do you not think on reflection, my friend, that you're being too harsh on Rothschild? Perhaps he doesn't fully understand what we seek to achieve," and adding as if as an afterthought, "after all, we will need the support of the great financiers of Europe."

"That's true, and I have to admit that it was the refusal of the baron to give the support I so earnestly needed that prompted the summoning of tomorrow's Congress. I'd humbled myself when I told him that if he refused to help then everything for which I'd worked would collapse. But refuse he did, and our objective must now be to motivate mass Jewish opinion."

The room was alive with the expectancy of what might happen the following day as Herzl spoke again, "and let me tell you, my dear friends, I will dress in my best, formally in evening suit with white tie."

Nordau looked at Herzl with a little surprise. "I read the request to those attending to dress formally, but somehow I didn't take it too seriously and I'm not sure that I'll comply. Please tell me why this strange stipulation?" Herzl began shaking his head. "Ah, you don't understand. This is an important occasion. We must first convince ourselves and then the Jewish people that we're serious about our proposals. Even though it is August, men who dress in summer clothing, and women in holiday apparel, will simply not send a message of solemnity. This is not a fashion display, but a new beginning for our people, and we must act, speak and dress as if it is so."

"My fear, Dr. Herzl, is that it'll prevent many from attending who might otherwise wish to do so, either because they are resistant or simply cannot afford an evening suit for which they may have no further use. This really is an unnecessary requirement to dress up as if we were going to the opera."

"We shall see," said Herzl, with a look which made it clear he considered the discussion closed. It hadn't gone unnoticed that he hadn't responded to Nordau's comments about the financial consideration.

Herzl rose to signal the meeting was at an end, and as I left the gathering I was filled with excitement and apprehension about my visit to Basel, where I felt destined to witness one of the great events in Jewish history.

CHAPTER SEVEN

Basel, Switzerland, 1897

It was August 28, 1897, and the weather in Basel was very hot, even for the time of year. We're staying in the Drei Könige Hotel located on Blumenrain, a hotel which was nearly 900 years old and had hosted Voltaire, Napoleon, Metternich and Charles Dickens. I'm not surprised by the visits by the former three as Basel sits at the junction of France, Germany and Switzerland, three countries which have either played home to generations of Jews or taken an influential role in Jewish history. Herzl had arrived on August 25, four days before the start of the Zionist Congress, to personally supervise and ensure that every detail of the arrangements was perfect. It was now the day before and he'd gone in the morning to the Stadtcasino, the Municipal Casino which housed the Concert Hall, the location of the Congress, and had returned in the early evening, looking excited.

"Would you care for an evening walk and perhaps a coffee or drink," I inquired, "or would you prefer to retire to prepare yourself for tomorrow's opening of the Congress?"

"Certainly not," came the reply with an uncharacteristic snort, "I couldn't possibly go to bed feeling as I do, enthusiastic and full of expectation for the outcome of this historic occasion. In any case, let Nordau retire early, he has to make the major speech."

So once again I'd enjoyed the privilege of sharing some private moments with this great man, Theodor Herzl, discussing his motives, expectations and even the odd disappointment. We left the hotel, crossed the Blumenrain and began our stroll through the narrow cobbled streets of this ancient city, glancing up at the brightly colored buildings which reflected the mixture of Gothic, Renaissance and Baroque periods. We walked through Fischmarkt and were in Spalenberg when Herzl pointed through a small archway at No. 12, to a cobbled courtyard, where we could just see a building with a two-tier balcony. He explained, "that is a very old place of entertainment called Theatre Fauteuil, which I suppose has about 100 seats and was, I believe, the home of a founder of the Dreyfus Bank, one of the oldest in Switzerland." We walked up the incline to reach Heuberg and turned into Unterer Heuberg, where many of the buildings dated back to the 14th and 15th centuries. We paused momentarily outside the sites of two former synagogues with shuttered windows in all the upper floors.

"Tell me, Dr Herzl, why did you choose Basel for the Zionist Congress?"

"I didn't. The first choice of the planning committee was Munich, although I must admit I didn't support the proposal. To our surprise, the Jewish communities of the city raised such objections that it would've been impossible to proceed. The opposition came from both the Orthodox and the Reform leaders. Although this was a disappointment, I realized very quickly that, as is often the case with the Jewish people, the opposition to making progress on almost any issue comes as much from within our community as from outside."

I had to admit that this judgment was one with which I was in complete agreement, and I couldn't help but speculate how different history might have been if Jews could have brought themselves to agree with one another, rather than argue all the time.

"I then considered Zürich and wrote to a Jewish lawyer, David Farbstein, to seek his advice. He'd only recently become a Swiss citizen and had been a Zionist from his early years, probably even before I embraced Zionism. With his brother he founded a Zionist youth organization and, not surprisingly, he was quick to reply recommending the city of Basel."

It seemed to me that this was to turn out to be a historic decision, not just because of the number of Zionist Congresses which would take place in Basel, but because of the welcome which Herzl and his supporters received and which was confirmed by his next words.

"We've been welcomed by the Jewish and wider communities, the City Council has made available its main concert hall as well as some office space just around the corner in Freie Strasse, and I'm optimistic that the president of the council, Dr Speiser, will attend our Congress."

"What about attendance? I know you don't wish to forecast, but how many do you expect and will they be sufficiently representative of the wider Jewish world to have any impact?"

"I cannot be certain until the registrations are complete, but I'll be disappointed if the numbers fall below 200. But, it's not the numbers that are important, it's the bringing together of like-minded Jews with a common vision to establish our state in Eretz Israel. I expect them to come from around sixteen countries and to include some non-Jewish supporters of the Zionist cause. It will send a strong symbol of our commitment – particularly to those wealthy Jewish families here in Europe and in England – that our movement is gathering pace, and we'll fulfill our ambitions if we're determined and united. Arranging this gathering was no easy task. When we announced our intention last March it was met with an outcry by those who sought to defeat our aspirations, but we've prevailed and I'm grateful to those who have stood by me, none less than Max Nordau."

I could sense his will to succeed, and demonstrate to those who had either opposed him or merely looked on, that Zionism would bring about the Herzl dream. He found it difficult to disguise his disappointment with the Rothschild and Hirsch families whose support he had so hoped to receive, and which would have made the task so much easier.

"I have to admit that my powers of persuasion were simply not strong enough to convince either of the barons of the need for their support, and whilst Hirsch is dead, it may still not be too late to engage with Rothschild whose financial support for Jews in despair has always been so generous. What did encourage me was a letter I received when I took a short rest at Aussee exactly twelve months ago."

We were walking past the Great Synagogue in Leimenstrasse, when he paused as we both took in the beauty of the stone and the elegant Byzantine cupolas. The synagogue, which had been built only thirty years earlier, had been expanded within the last few years. "It may surprise you, but I attended the Sabbath service and then I was surprised when I was called to witness the reading from the scroll of the Holy Torah by my Hebrew name Binyamin Ze'ev ben Ya'acov. Donning the prayer shawl and participating in the service is not something I've done since my bar mitzva, and I admit I found the experience very moving." With a smile on his face he quietly added, "I was certainly more nervous than I felt about addresseing the Congress."

Herzl's reference to his bar mitzva seemed to cause him to gaze longingly at the synagogue as if in a dream, his mind wandering back into the past. Suddenly he turned to me, speaking in a quiet voice. "I'm sorry if my mind appears to have wandered, but when I recall the time of my bar mitzva I'm reminded of a strange dream I had around that time. I've told few about this experience for fear of being accused of being, how shall I say, something of a heretic. In this dream I saw the Messiah sweeping all before him including me, as we rested on pure white clouds. Sitting on one of these clouds was a figure I took to be Moses, resembling in my mind Michelangelo's statue. In a conversation between the two characters of my dream the suggestion was made that I, Theodor Herzl, would perform some great deed which would benefit not only the Jewish people, but the whole world."

He looked at me to see if I was still listening to what might be regarded as a bizarre revelation, as I too reflected on the image of Moses as I wondered at this amazing prophesy in Herzl's dream.

It was to be more than a century later when I personally saw the interior of this elegant synagogue. It seemed to have been designed to blend with the city's architecture, and the fine interior with its Moorish influence was dominated by the impressive ark which held the Torah scrolls, adorned with beautiful mantles and polished silver artifacts. I realized that my mind was wandering and I should revert to reminding Herzl about the letter he'd just spoken about.

"This letter you mention, who was it from?" I asked gently.

"Ah yes, thank you. It was from the chief rabbi of Paris, Zadoc Kahn, and he proposed that we convene a meeting of the larger Jewish communities; indeed, he suggested that it should be in secret. I think he was aware of the differences between Rothschild and me, and felt that we should not alienate him any further. Whilst I understood the rabbi's good intentions, I rejected the idea because – as you will see tomorrow – it's important that we demonstrate our intentions in a spectacular and memorable style. So we'll assemble in a casino, perhaps a strange location for our purpose, but I'm optimistic that history will judge the debate and deliberations with more kindness than the venue. I hope this will be the case as much for Nordau as anyone else, for he's worked unceasingly to achieve a successful Congress."

It was obvious that to have actually reached this point with the first formal Zionist gathering about to start, it had required outstanding diplomatic skills on Herzl's part.

"I can well appreciate that you must have faced widespread opposition to convening this Congress – especially as there are those who feel that Zionism has been a movement in existence for some years when one recalls that Nathan Birnbaum wrote about the concept some nine years ago – and that perhaps you are trying to change Jewish history."

Herzl looked at me with a stern gaze before replying. "Of course, that's exactly what I'm trying to do. Those committed to the Zionist cause have been too relaxed in their efforts. They have talked too much and acted too little, with the result that we've made no progress. I'm trying to change Jewish history and, to-morrow, that is what we'll achieve."

We turned to start our return to the hotel, passing the Stadthof Hotel, turning into Gerbergasse – another narrow street towards Marktplatz, which had only just been redesigned. The square was dominated by the town hall and surrounded by many newly built typically European buildings, with balconies and wrought-iron balustrades. We carefully avoided a horse trough spilling water onto the clean footways and as we approached the river bank we could see considerable building activity, as the port on the Rhine was taking shape.

"This is indeed a great city, going through a period of huge change with a heavy program of new construction. The German-speaking population is sophisticated and expanding very quickly. Before I arrived I'd heard about how set in their ways the people are, and I trust they made you welcome."

"Indeed they have, and the Swiss reputation for calm efficiency has made our task that much more simple," came Herzl's reply.

We'd been walking for some fifty minutes and, returning to the hotel, decided to sit and drink before retiring to bed. A waiter took our orders and as he scurried away to the bar I was surprised to see Herzl remove from his pocket some postcards which he showed me, explaining that they were to commemorate the Congress. He hoped to find time to send them to his children. For someone who did not speak often about his family I found this touching.

"My wife and children are visiting their grandmother. Sadly, I have to confess that both she and the late Herr Naschauer, my father-in-law, who died after a long illness, have never fully ap-proved of my aims and wouldn't consider themselves Zionists."

It seemed an appropriate time to leave Herzl to his own thoughts as he contemplated what the next few days might bring to him, to the Jewish people, indeed to the whole world.

*   *   *

I awoke the next morning to hear considerable activity in the corridor and, dressing quickly, I left Room 126 to take some breakfast. I walked a few paces and saw Theodor Herzl leaning on the balcony rail outside Room 122 as he gazed across the River Rhine at the eastern side of the city. I suspected that the famous picture of him may well have been taken on any of the early occasions that the Zionist Congress was held in Basel.

"Good morning. It's a fine day as we set off in a new chapter of our 5,000 years of history. You'll accompany me, I trust, to the Stadtcasino to witness the debate and hopefully the adoption of our resolutions. I cannot believe that you'll be bored by those who speak, but if that should be the case, let me give you a copy of *Die Welt* to peruse. This is the eleventh issue and it began its weekly life only in June when I decided to publish a Zionist weekly paper," he smiled mischievously, as he added, "partly to publicize this Congress."

Taking the folded paper I thought how could I possibly admit to him that such an experience – to be a fly on the auditorium wall – would have been the wish of every Jew with even the slightest Zionist aspiration in generations to follow. I felt deeply privileged to share such an opportunity.

We walked through the Barfüsserplatz, arriving at Basel's Municipal Casino within a few minutes. The building, in the shadow of the Barfüsser Church fronting on to Steinenberg, was relatively simple with an imposing entrance over which hung a banner reading "Zionistkongress" with a star of David above. The impressive foyer, from which marble stairs rose to the upper floors, and the congress halls were decorated as if a festival was being celebrated. Herzl excused himself to ensure that everything was in order. He'd no intention of leaving to chance even the smallest detail. I took my seat in the balcony and looked around the gray unadorned walls of the Congress Hall before concentrating on the assembled delegates. I was unsure if we were in the main hall because of the limited numbers, although I suspected that Herzl would have insisted on the use of the great concert hall.

I was surprised how many appeared to have acceded to Herzl's request to attend in formal dress and the national differences were not always apparent. It was easy to identify the elegance of the Scandinavians and English, the more casual appearance of the Americans, the total correctness of the Austrians and Germans, and the attempts to "dress up" by the masses from Russia, Rumania and Bulgaria. The delegates from Palestine had made an attempt to comply, but clearly felt that formal dress was not a prerequisite to the establishment of a Jewish State. There was a sprinkling of ladies among the audience, all of whom were elegantly dressed, and this added a touch of feminine color to what the journalists present might have described as a rather dour crowd of people. I studied the audience more closely, having learned that there were just twenty-one women delegates, and it was obvious that many of those present were only in their twenties and thirties.

The top table, fairly long on a raised dais and covered in green cloth, had a slightly higher chair for the president which would be occupied temporarily by a Dr. Lippe, who would open the Congress. The platform party was seated in what appeared to be a two- or three-tiered layout which reminded me, rather unkindly, of the older British Conservative Party conferences where the platform party sat in tiers to indicate order of importance. There appeared to be a delay, which I thought would irritate Herzl, who had striven so hard to ensure that the program ran exactly to time. I learned later that this was because Max Nordau had arrived without the requested evening dress, and reconsidered after some argument, and then only because Herzl had urged him: "Nordau, for my sake if for no other reason, please change into evening dress, for you and I must set an example to Jews throughout the world that we're serious about the objectives of this Congress."

Nordau relented and returned to the hotel to change.

And so the First Zionist Congress opened, just a little late, on Sunday, August 29, 1897, in the presence of some 200 attendees, sixty-nine appointed representatives of Zionist societies and the remainder specially invited, including a handful of non-Jewish guests.

The Congress president, Dr. Karl Lippe, banged the gavel three times on the table and as he rose a silence spread through the entire audience. He covered his head and began to recite the traditional Hebrew prayer asking God to bless a new festival or new experience, and as he did so the delegates rose too, joining him quietly and solemnly, *"shehechiyanu, vekiyemanu, vehigiyanu lazman hazeh"* ["who has kept us alive, sustained us and brought us to this season"]. Dr. Lippe waited for us all to be seated, and as he invited Dr. Herzl to the podium, the hall rose as one to greet him with sustained applause. which must have lasted more than fifteen minutes. My mind raced forward a hundred years as I re-called how British prime ministers, and presumably American presidents too, were also welcomed to their party conferences with enthusiastic applause which always seemed so organized. Not so the welcome for Theodor Herzl, which was entirely spon-taneous.

Herzl looked around at what he had described as a historic gathering and calmly and without emotion spoke.

"We are here to lay the cornerstone of the house which is to shelter the Jewish Nation. Zionism is the return of the Jewish people to Judaism before their return to the Jewish land. We have already achieved something remarkable by bringing together the extremes of Judaism, the traditionally Orthodox and the modern reformers, and that's a union which can only bring success."

I couldn't help wonder about these words coming from a man who had in so many ways faced up to the needs of where Jews would live whilst turning his back on their spiritual needs. It was a discussion I promised myself to have with him at a later date, perhaps when we viewed the lifestyle of the modern Israeli.

There were other speakers and the man, who captured my attention and that of all the delegates, was Max Nordau, for when he reached the podium, his distinguished stature commanded the hall. He was a powerful orator who referred only briefly to his notes. He spoke of Jewish misery, of anti-Semitism and emancipation, and he ranged far and wide across the continent of Europe as he described the distress of the Jewish people. "Jewish distress has two forms," Nordau claimed, "material and moral. In Eastern Europe, North Africa and Western Asia, where the vast majority of our people live, the misery of the Jews is clear – it is the daily distress of the body, anxiety about the next day and the fight for the existence and security of life. In Western Europe the struggle is less, though I see it growing. Here, the question of food and shelter is less of a problem, whilst the misery is moral." He went on to quote the words, "the Western Jew has bread, but man does not live on bread alone." I listened carefully as he singled out England with such conviction and truth. "The English people will not allow its progress to be influenced from outside, emancipation here is a living thing and not just written about. This is a great nation with respect for its traditions, and where society with a spiritual life does not recognize the difference between Christian and Jew, and that's why there are few incidences of anti-Semitism."

We then heard Nordau's views about the ghetto mentality of the Jew, how the word "ghetto" symbolized in some minds shame and humiliation and was seen as a prison, whereas to others it was built by the Jew himself and not for him. It was a refuge for his protection and survival. Nordau then returned to a principal theme of anti-Semitism. "Through the ages, the Jew saw himself as French, German or Italian. Anti-Semitism is again breaking out, the Jew may be allowed to vote for members of parliament and discharge his duties as a citizen, but is excluded from being a member of the clubs and meetings which are the province of the majority

Christian population. In Western Europe he's given up his natural Jewish characteristics, left behind the ghetto, but the land of his birth is still denied as his home." Here was Nordau's message, and he finished with rousing words. "Jewish distress cried for help and it is the work of this Congress to answer that cry."

It was Nordau's committee which proposed the adoption of the Basel Program stating that "the aim of Zionism is to establish a home for the Jewish people in Eretz Israel secured by law". The assembly went on to discuss how to achieve this objective, and finally agreed a four-point plan which included "the promotion of the colonization of Palestine by Jewish agricultural and industrial workers, binding together world Jewry and the strengthening of Jewish national sentiment and consciousness." What impressed me was that the Basel Program was established on a foundation of obtaining government consent, and in accordance with the laws of each country.

The tone of the Congress was set and Herzl proceeded to guide and control it, with natural and impeccable skill. He gained the respect of all present, as he used his diplomacy to avoid confrontation and, by the use of the right word and gesture at the right time, brought just the right atmosphere to the occasion. There was much debate about the resolution and particularly about clarification of "law" and finally on Herzl's personal recommendation the words "secured by public law" were adopted.

We listened carefully to the words of David Farbstein, who described the economic reasons for the Zionist objectives. This was followed by Nathan Birnbaum, another example of the vibrant delegates in their thirties, who explained cultural needs. Born in Vienna, and brought up in an assimilated community, he compared the differences between the Eastern and Western Jews, and the urgency of each beginning to understand the other if they were to successfully live together.

One speaker who came to the podium was clearly a rabbi. He was, I estimated, in his thirties, bearded and with a typical Eastern European square skullcap. I quietly asked a delegate who this might be. "That, my friend, is Rabbi Arthur Cohn of the Basel Jewish Community, indeed the first appointed rabbi, and it's largely through his efforts that this Congress is taking place here. Unlike many of his rabbinical colleagues, he's become an enthusiastic Zionist and succeeded in convincing the community leaders of the merits of hosting this event here." Our conversation was interrupted by the rabbi's question which asked, understandably, whether the new Jewish state would strictly observe the Sabbath. Herzl's reply would have set an example to every aspiring politician when he assured the audience, and the rabbi, that Zionism would do nothing to upset any section of the Jewish people. I was surprised that this response drew such applause.

In the closing speech, Prof. Max Mandelstamm thanked Herzl for his courage and drive which had succeeded, probably for the first time in centuries, in bringing together from the four quarters of the Jewish world such an assembly which had set Jewish history on a new course. Herzl closed the First Congress to the delight and joy of all who attended, and was elected president of the World Zionist Organization.

As I waited for Herzl to emerge from the Municipal Hall, so we could walk back together to the Drei Könige Hotel, I reflected on my return visit to Basel a little over a century later. I found a clean city with a disappointing mix of new buildings with old, where the modernity of the glass structures somehow clashed, rather than blended, with the city's history. The city remained busy and bustling with the noise and screech of trams, which first appeared just two years before the 1897 Congress, criss-crossing the streets providing an efficient, if not a little dangerous, mode of travel to those without their wits about them.

Herzl emerged onto the street, looking distinctly exhausted, and said nothing for several minutes. I felt it inappropriate to interrupt his private thoughts.

Suddenly he turned to me. "We've had a triumph. The Congress has surpassed my wildest dreams. Even without the great Jewish magnates, we've harnessed the strength of the masses and lit a fire which will burn until our National Home becomes a reality. Just observe the number of journalists who attended, and not from insignificant journals, but the *New York Herald,* the *Frankfurter Zeitung, L'Echo de Paris* and your very own London *Times.* Plus, of course, the Hebrew press and *Jewish Chronicle."*

"Indeed it's been truly magnificent, and for those who were present to witness the results, they'll dream about it and recount the experience to their children and grandchildren." I paused before asking, "Dr. Herzl, if you had to sum up the achievement, how would you describe it?"

He appeared pensive before replying. "I'm unsure that I would say this in public, but I might say that here in Basel *I founded the Jewish State.* If I was to say this out loud I might be laughed at, but perhaps in five years, certainly in fifty, everyone will know it."

As we turned into the hotel, and with the benefit of foresight, I couldn't believe how prophetic Herzl's statement was to be.

CHAPTER EIGHT

Constantinople, Turkey, 1898

It was Monday evening, October 3, 1898, and I was in the audience at a meeting in the East End of London, waiting with thousands of others for Herzl to mount the stage. As he arrived, the audience, which some reports claimed numbered 7,000, while others stated 10,000, erupted into spontaneous applause. He waited patiently for the welcome to subside.

"We've had another outstanding Zionist Congress in Basel, twice the number of delegates as the first meeting, and what a delight for me to welcome my father as a delegate. I'm full of enthusiasm for the task ahead. I believe that the time is fast approaching when the Jewish people will be on the march."

With these opening words – even though delivered quietly in German – Herzl wooed his audience comprising mainly the traditional Jewish working classes who were looking for inspired leadership. His dream, to set up a National Home for the Jews in Palestine, flew in the face of the Orthodox rabbinical preaching which claimed that this would only come about when the Messiah arrived. Following the meeting, as we returned to the hotel, he expressed his delight with the gathering and how it had given him just the spur he needed.

What excited me was that later in the month, Herzl would make his first visit to Palestine and I'd accompany him on this pioneering experience.

* * *

I found myself in the opulent surroundings of the Orient Express, only recently renamed from "Express d'Orient," as it sped through the European countryside from Vienna, the start of our journey to Constantinople, our first port of call. I'd admitted my relief that within recent years the line had been extended so as to avoid the uncomfortable sea journey from Varna in Bulgaria, across the Black Sea, to Constantinople. The train had started its journey in Paris and for those who were to experience the whole journey, they'd be on the train for almost three days.

Herzl suggested we might visit the dining car, and as we took our seats we were joined at an adjacent table by four other men, all of them in my view of a similar age to Herzl himself and sporting similar beards.

"May I introduce Herren Max Bodenheimer, David Wolffsohn, Josef Seidener and Dr. Moses Schnirer, who are accompanying me on this vital mission." We shook hands, and as they spoke in German I had to rely on some interpretation to understand what was being said.

"These gentlemen have between them a range of skills essential to achieving our objectives. Herr Bodenheimer is a lawyer, and we certainly need his eye for the meticulous detail of any submission we might make; Herr Wolffsohn and Herr Seidener have considerable experience in the fields of finance and the purchase of land; and Dr. Schnirer, who is a vice president of the Zionist Organization, is by good fortune a physician – so that if one of us should fall ill, we have our own medical adviser!"

Everyone laughed as the dining-car steward presented some menus, which then occupied the next ten minutes of discussion as the choice of wine was debated at length. I found the menu somewhat ambitious for my taste so I settled for some fruit and cheese, with a glass of wine chosen by those more experienced than me.

I then became a mere onlooker as the four men began to discuss what was happening in the world. Herzl looked at me before starting to speak. "You'll recall that we met with Madame Dreyfus in Paris. Well, earlier this year Major Esterhazy was tried at a military tribunal and unbelievably acquitted on charges of treason, although it was clear he was the culprit. As if this were not bad enough, the well- known author Emile Zola, writing in *L'Aurore*, had penned an article under the headline 'J'accuse', which proclaimed Dreyfus's innocence and, as a result, *he* was then tried for libel and imprisoned."

"Doesn't that just reflect the culture of anti-Semitism which prevails in France?" said Seidener, and as the discussion progressed Wolffsohn added, "But the culmination of the sorry story is the confession of perjury by a French colonel, Henri Piquart, who was sent to prison and committed suicide."

"If that were the end of the saga, it would be of some satisfaction, but whilst Dreyfus sits on Devil's Island, there can be no peace for any of us."

The conversation moved on to expressions of shock about recent events in Kiev, Russia, where several thousand Jews had been driven from their homes. It was Josef Seidener who spoke, his voice rising in obvious anger and attracting glances from other travelers. "I feel so inadequate when I hear this news, for how can we be surprised when it's the wretched culmination of years of the oppression, rape and murder of our people. The pogroms right across Russia and particularly in Kiev, as well as Podolia, Odessa and Volhynia, have set a pattern of anti-Semitism which we can only hope won't be replicated in other European countries."

"Sadly, there's already news from Warsaw of similar acts of violence," said Schnirer. "Perhaps the world, which stands by and watches – particularly the Jewish world – will come to realize how necessary is the foundation of our own home, for these acts are contagious. I'm shocked by the desecration of our synagogues, homes and Jewish owned stores." His words drew nods of agreement from all those around the table.

"You refer to the world standing by..." interrupted Herzl. "When I was last in London there were public protests, even the Lord Mayor of London made a direct approach to the czar, and when he was prime minister, Mr. Gladstone had expressed regret and disgust with these activities."

"The Americans have added their voice of concern through their ambassador in Russia, and in New York there've been major demonstrations, but now that Gladstone has died I wonder what the effect will be of the British government's protestations?" These words from Max Bodenheimer seemed to silence the discussion, and as we all retired to our own private thoughts to consider the terrible happenings in Eastern Europe, the steward arrived to set the food on the table. A glass of wine was poured and it seemed to my inexperienced palate to be more than acceptable.

"So what else has been happening in this troubled world of ours?" came a question from the table.

"The Spanish-American War has now been under way for six months, and it was entirely predictable when their warship *Maine* was sunk in Havana Harbor. The map of the world is undergoing change with the United States annexing Cuba, Puerto Rico and the Philippines."

The physician at the table, Dr. Schnirer, had a contrasting aspect of world events to share.

"There's tragic news from China, where a terrible bubonic plague has broken out and I fear millions will die. But by contrast, I hear that Madame Marie Curie, with her husband, Pierre, is on the verge of announcing their discovery of radium and this will have a huge benefit on medical science for generations to come."

"It's surprising how so often, out of some tragedy, goodness can result," said Bodenheimer. "The tragic assassination last month in Geneva of the empress of Austria brought an array of distinguished mourners to the city, and our friend, the Rev.

Hechler, delivered a particularly stirring sermon to the congregation. Following that he wrote to the grand duke of Baden, lauding Theodor's views about the Holy Land. As if that were not enough, the kaiser himself, during his visit to Geneva for the funeral, spent some time in the small Palestine Museum which Hechler had established in the Embassy."

"What was the result of that?" inquired Wolffson.

"Ah, that's where the good fortune arises, for the kaiser was due to visit Palestine, and the museum experience, brief as it was, had excited him about his forthcoming journey."

"Interesting, as, presumably that's why the kaiser is making such a holy journey?" enquired someone around the table.

"That too is interesting, because it's to attend the dedication of the Evangelist Church of the Redeemer built by the Germans. I know that His Majesty is anxious to increase his country's influence, particularly in offering his protection to the German Catholics."

"That's understandable," came a response, "because they're anxious to reduce the French influence, which always seems to produce diplomatic problems."

As we continued to enjoy our meal, I turned to Herzl and asked him quietly, "Tell me, what do *you* seek from this visit to Constantinople and Palestine?"

He seemed pleased with the question, which provided an opportunity to return the conversation to his vision. Herzl recalled his meeting with the German ambassador in Vienna, Count Philipp Eulenburg, a trusted confidant of the kaiser. "It was a warm and friendly encounter and Eulenberg expressed the hope that perhaps Germany would replace England as the natural sponsor of the Zionist aspiration, and offer German protection of the National Home."

This suggestion fell on my ears with considerable surprise. I suspected that their motives might not have been as pure as Herzl thought; The desire to rid Germany of some of the more unacceptable Jewish citizens was certainly an incentive. I also had the benefit of foresight and realized how much the German attitude to all Jews during the Nazi period had changed in less than forty years.

"He couldn't arrange an immediate meeting with the kaiser, but did offer to introduce me to Bernhard von Bülow, the foreign secretary, an offer I grasped with enthusiasm – although I readily admit I didn't find the atmosphere at this meeting as relaxing as with the ambassador. But I did secure an important promise – von Bülow agreed that I could address the German delegation in Jerusalem, provided my draft was agreed in advance in Constantinople. I'd received a wonderful letter from Eulenberg at the end of last month. He told me that both the kaiser and von Bülow understood our cause and were supportive of it, and as if that weren't good enough news, he also told me that His Majesty would be prepared to intervene with the sultan on our behalf."

"That's excellent news," said Bodenheimer, "and *that*, I suspect, is the driving force for this journey."

"Exactly, because the kaiser is offering to receive a Zionist deputation in Jerusalem. He suggested that I should lead it, and present our case. But my dear friends, I must ask for your absolute discretion as it is considered that such a meeting, if it were held in Germany, and possibly even in Palestine, could give rise to even more objections than those already expressed about his forthcoming visit."

Herzl's four associates all indicated that his secret was safe with them, and asked if he was aware of the kaiser's program.

"The main party arrives in Constantinople tomorrow, on October 17, and sails for Haifa on the 25th. My understanding is that the voyage takes about three days and they'll be in Jerusalem from October 29 until they depart a week later. That's why our own timescale is so critical. This is an opportunity which may not occur again, and I mustn't miss it."

The railway guard walked through the carriage announcing that the train was approaching Belgrade, where there would be a brief stop.

"Before we all retire," said Herzl, "there's an important issue to which we must apply our minds, and that's the amount of land we would require and how we would determine the boundaries and borders. This is absolutely vital to our future. Seidener, we need your views on this."

It was Bodenheimer who offered the first suggestion. "We should seek the area from the Brook of Egypt to the River Euphrates."

As I listened to the debate on the land issue, my mind raced ahead in time as I thought about the significance of the borders and the impact this was to have on the Arab neighbors, and the rest of the world. It was only within twenty or so years before Herzl's visit that the first wave of some 25,000 Zionist immigrants from Eastern Europe had been permitted to settle in Palestine by the Ottoman government. They'd been supported by Baron Edmond de Rothschild's financial backing for Jewish colonization, and herein lay the problem. Whilst the Ottomans initially allowed pilgrims and businessmen to visit the Holy Land, they were less than happy about Zionist colonization and indeed later banned foreign Jewish businessmen altogether.

Seidener took up the challenge of the land. "Let us look to the heights of Mount Hermon in the north, across the desert of the Negev towards the Red Sea in the south."

I returned to my compartment in the company of Herzl and reflected on the conversation.

"Will you not face a huge opposition from the Ottomans and the surrounding Arab nations, and won't their numbers simply overwhelm the Jewish State you seek to establish? It's only in recent times that the Cairo newspaper *al-Manar* has warned about the Zionist ambitions and your aim to take possession in Palestine."

"It's true that the sultan, Abdul Hamid, has rejected my proposals and has sent members of his own staff to govern Jerusalem. That's why I need the kaiser's support and the opportunity to explain to the sultan in a personal hearing that we mean no threat to the Arab nations, or indeed those who currently live within the existing borders."

The train steamed into the Sirkeci station at Constantinople for what was to be Herzl's second visit to the city, and two years on, the train journey had made far less of an impression on him than his first. As we climbed down on to the platform, the passengers were greeted by uniformed dragomans, described to me as interpreters and guides sent from the various embassies to ensure their citizens safely reached their hotels. Like all great stations of the period, Sirkeci was a magnificent building in true oriental style.

There were disappointments awaiting the party, as the German Embassy was obstructing the interview promised by von Bülow; however they underestimated Herzl's persistent character. The interview was finally arranged at the last moment on the day after our arrival, October 18, and just before the German party sailed for Alexandria prior to their onward journey to Jaffa.

"It was a most inspiring meeting," confided Herzl to me in a whisper as he recalled his meeting with Kaiser Wilhelm II. "He was dressed just as I imagined a German emperor would dress. His hussar uniform was pressed and appeared as if he wore each uniform only once. I was so delighted that I too had decided to dress for the occasion and felt comfortable in the new frock coat I had acquired for the meeting. He was majestic in so many ways, and although I suspected that he was concealing his withered arm, he stood boldly with fine features capped by a mustache which turned up at the ends and didn't hide his smile. "I had invited Herr Wolffsohn to accompany me and I introduced him to the kaiser, who had welcomed us at the door of his rooms, and then to von Bülow. I'd heard that the emperor had suffered a brain tumor, which was likely to cause him to be aggressive, with strange behavioral traits, but he appeared warm and outwardly friendly. We discussed anti-Semitism in Germany and in Europe as well as our mutual opinion of the French, and at the end of the conversation – which I felt at one stage was slipping away from us – the kaiser asked the one question I had hoped for: 'What would you like me to say to the sultan?'"

He paused, as if reflecting on whether he had given the right reply.

"I felt deeply that the only way we would achieve our homeland was by political means and we needed the support and yes, the approval of the international community. The role of Germany was crucial and, what's more, the only country who might be able to influence Turkey to negotiate with us."

"I'm not sure what you consider your negotiating strengths," I ventured quietly.

"Turkey has severe fiscal problems and I'd hoped that in exchange for Jewish financial support the government could be persuaded to grant us some land in Palestine."

"So what was your reply to the kaiser?"

"I asked simply for a Jewish state under German protection." Herzl appeared not to notice the look of surprise on my face. "One of the suggestions considered was the formation of a chartered company along the lines of Cecil Rhodes's British Chartered Company in South Africa, established successfully under Queen Victoria, to encourage the colonization of Rhodesia."

And so we left Constantinople for Palestine, a historic journey, and an experience I was about to share with one of the greatest personalities in Jewish history.

CHAPTER NINE

Jerusalem, Palestine, 1898

Early morning, October 26, 1898. Our ship had left Port Said the previous evening, not before our party, especially Herzl, had looked on with amazement at the Suez Canal. He quietly confessed to being more impressed by the water of the canal stretching away into the distance than by the Acropolis. The 100-mile canal, connecting the Mediterranean and Red seas, and completed some thirty years earlier, was now open to ships of every country and technically owned by the British government.

I had joined Herzl on the deck of the ship, appropriately named *Russia*, bringing us on the last stage of our journey from Alexandria to Jaffa. We wanted to witness this first sight of the Holy Land. As we strained our eyes, Herzl, wearing a kind of sea captain's cap and appearing somewhat disheveled as if he had spent most of the night on the deck of the ship, stretched out his arm pointing with excitement. "Look, my friend, there is Jaffa. See the minarets which dominate the skyline. What a wonderful sight."

I couldn't help but turn to look at him, and saw that his whole body was standing erect with a glow on his face, reflecting the emerging sun as it began to shine on the buildings of Jaffa. We'd been joined on the deck by David Wolffsohn who, uncharacteristically, put his arm around Herzl's shoulder as they gazed at the land for which they had so much hope and optimism. It was a memorable moment and one to cherish forever, as other passengers joined us to look at the sight which had been denied to so many. I looked at the makeup of those peering over the ship's railings: several in traditional Arab dress, others clearly from an Eastern European background.

We were kept waiting on board until the kaiser's royal party had disembarked, and then were ferried to the shore in a Thomas Cook launch. As we walked ashore we were greeted by crowds of onlookers, who were prevented from approaching the ship by German police. We were to be billeted at a hotel in Jaffa, an experience which attracted me rather less than Herzl. But, it was setting foot on the soil of Eretz Israel which made everything else appear rather unimportant. The following morning Herzl, who had become unwell on the ship, seemed no better, but he rose early to plan his meeting with the kaiser. He'd decided to visit some agricultural settlements, and asked if I'd like to accompany him. We traveled the few miles from Jaffa to Rishon Lezion, which had been supported by the Rothschilds for some fourteen years and was now a thriving oasis of vines spreading across 2,000 acres.

"I think we should return to the hotel," said Herzl, "I find the heat oppressive and I must be at my best when we encounter His Majesty." I agreed with this as he seemed quite exhausted, and together we made our way back to our hotel where our rooms just barely sheltered us from the noise and activity which dominated the building.

"Tomorrow, my friend, we'll meet with the kaiser's party and we must be up early so as not to miss the opportunity."

"And where, Dr. Herzl, will this meeting take place?"

"We will place ourselves on the road near to the entrance to the settlement Mikveh Israel, which is not far from Jaffa. The German group is due to visit and learn about this agricultural school. I have asked Eulenburg's cousin, who is the kaiser's court official, to make His Majesty aware of my presence."

Mikveh Israel, which means "The Hope of Israel," seemed an entirely appropriate location for this meeting, as it accurately reflected Herzl's dream. It had been founded by the French organization Alliance Israelite Universelle some twenty years earlier. It seemed ironic to me that we stood outside the place funded by the body so generously supported by Baron Hirsch, which had been so opposed to Herzl's ideas.

The following morning, accompanied by Herzl's travelling companions, we stationed ourselves on the roadway close to the school. I was of course not surprised that Herzl, despite his continuing fever, was dressed formally and with considerable care. He expressed his customary criticism of those who hadn't taken similar trouble. We'd been standing for about forty minutes in the shade of the palm trees, planted with the objective of draining the swamps, and amongst a small crowd of onlookers, a mix of Arabs and Jews, men, women and children. Some were looking a little dazed about the whole experience and others with wild expectation, when we saw the kaiser's party approaching led by a troop of Turkish soldiers on horseback. The welcoming party was headed by some of the hundred students of Mikveh Israel and their director, Yosef Niego.

When Kaiser Wilhelm II stopped by our waiting group, Herzl stepped forward and, bowing respectfully, removed his pith helmet, which was taller than the traditional style resembling the military version of the helmet, synonymous with British colonialism. I was standing at the rear of the group and couldn't hear the brief conversation between the two men, which ended with a wave from the kaiser and a sweeping gesture from Herzl. We stood for a few moments, watching the Germans and their accompanying officials as the school's director introduced his members of staff and students, who sang the German National Anthem taught, it's been suggested, by Herzl himself. Herzl was anxious to thank Niego for helping to make his meeting possible, but as he was still suffering from a fever, he decided to write a note when he returned to Vienna.

Leaving this meeting, we traveled to Jerusalem by train and as we boarded, I noticed that Herzl didn't appear his usual self, with small beads of perspiration on his forehead. In reply to my question, he put his index finger to his lips. "I've had a mild fever since our arrival, perhaps brought on by the sea journey." I didn't feel that I should add that spending most of the night on the deck of the ship wouldn't have helped. It was Friday afternoon and the Sabbath was fast approaching and the group decided to walk to the hotel rather than ride. I'm not sure this met with total agreement from Herzl, who clearly was feeling distinctly unwell, but didn't wish to encourage anyone to desecrate the Sabbath by riding to the hotel.

Herzl was shocked by the barren land, the lack of cultivation and care, and this only strengthened his resolve to bring Jewish enthusiasm and skills to make the land once again one of "milk and honey". Following our walk through the narrow streets of the Old City, Herzl turned to me, saying, "I'm not sure I'll recall this visit with total pleasure, as I feel the weight of 2,000 years of neglect, intolerance and inhumanity. Can't you smell the filth as we walk through the alleys?" As we visited the holy place of the Western Wall – the retaining wall of the surroundings of the destroyed Temple – he spoke of his wish to see "this unique example of Biblical history freed from the presence of beggars, and all of this dereliction pulled down and replaced by modern buildings with proper sewage for the benefit of the inhabitants." When I pressed him, he agreed that naturally the holy places of every religion would be preserved and these would remain untouched.

It was during our visit to Jerusalem that Herzl demonstrated further strength of character. Despite suggestions from other members of our party, he had resolutely refused to go the Temple Mount. "I feel that my lack of Orthodoxy somehow inhibits me from such a sacred visit." Later in the day, by contrast, he expressed a determination to walk along the Via Dolorosa, along which Jesus is believed to have walked from his trial to the place of his crucifixion, despite warnings about anti-Semitic threats from the

Christians living there. "I'll not be told where I can and where I cannot walk in this city of Jerusalem."

I thought about my more recent visits to Jerusalem and how the holy places of Christianity, Islam and Judaism had been preserved, and were still visited by thousands of pilgrims and worshippers each year.

The meeting with the kaiser in Palestine had been obstructed by nearly everyone with whom we came into contact; indeed it had been later suggested that the meeting never actually took place. Herzl's party was equally unwelcomed by the Jews as the Germans, and a number of international incidents, including one between France and Britain, threatened the whole process. Eventually we received news that our delegation should travel to an encampment where Wilhelm II and his foreign minister, von Bülow, would receive us in their tent. Herzl read his prepared statement but was devastated by the unexpected response from both the Emperor and his foreign minister.

"Dr. Herzl, we have listened carefully to your proposals for the colonization of Palestine as a national home for the Jewish people, but there is in our minds a more paramount objective."

Herzl listened carefully and respectfully, disappointed by the opening words and anticipating even worse as the kaiser continued. "What this land needs above all else is water and trees, to grow."

This is as far as the discussion got. The Zionist party retired with the distinct view that this visit to Palestine, rather than advance the Zionist ideal, had set it back in time particularly with the Germans, and subsequently with Herzl's real target, the mighty sultan, who reigned over so much of the Middle East.

As we left the encampment, Herzl turned to me and with typical optimism confided, "Come, it's time to depart from this place. We've been thwarted, but only temporarily, there's work to do and we'll return to Vienna with utmost speed."

That's how we found ourselves on the English four-masted ship *Dundee*, just sixteen years since being launched, as it sailed from Jaffa to Alexandria and onwards via Naples back to Vienna.

CHAPTER TEN

Vienna, Austria, 1902

October 1902, and I was once again in the elegant surroundings of the Sacher Hotel in Vienna, awaiting Herzl's arrival. Little had changed since my last visit to the Sacherstube café. Most of the tables were occupied, with well-dressed guests drinking coffee or chocolate and eating delicacies from china plates, whilst the maitre d' in his well-pressed morning suit with stiff white collar and tie moved silently around the room, in total command.

Herzl arrived shortly after I'd taken a seat and I stood and offered a hand of welcome, which he grasped warmly, even though he appeared tired and strained.

"It's good to see you after so much time, looking so well and here in Vienna. So much has happened in these last two or three years since we were last together in the Holy Land."

"Indeed so, and you'll forgive me if I say that you're looking a little tired."

I realized I was about to learn about his further journeys and exploits as he pursued his vision of a Jewish National Home, which was clearly taking a toll on his health.

"It's been a hard period, with much travel including Berlin, Paris and London, and, as I explained when we talked at the

Savoy Hotel, there have been rewarding experiences as well as disappointments. I met the Austrian prime minister, Herr Ernest von Koerber, on several occasions. Max Nordau introduced me to a Mr. Alfred Austin, who promised to give me a letter for your prime minister, Lord Salisbury; and perhaps the best of all, I spoke with a Hungarian, Arminius Vámbéry, in Budapest, who promised to write to the sultan with whom he claimed to be friendly." He paused long enough to suggest, "I'm talking too much, let's order some refreshment and then I'll bring you up to date with our news."

As if by telepathy, a waiter appeared at the table and quietly accepted our order for a coffee and cognac for Herzl, and a cup of the Sacher Hotel's delightful chocolate for me.

"Do you know who that is over there?" asked Herzl, pointing to a clean-shaven man with high forehead and in a heavy three-piece tweed suit and droopy bow tie. Not waiting for an answer, which would have been negative, he continued. "That's Gustav Mahler, the famous director of music at the Vienna Opera, with his new wife, the former Alma Schindler. They've just been joined by Richard Strauss, the composer."

"She's really lovely and so elegant," was all I could find to say as I sat admiring the young Viennese beauty, and I wasn't the only man in the room to quietly show appreciation. After my initial reaction, my attention was drawn to Mahler as he spoke with obvious passion, arms in the air as if conducting an orchestra.

"Is it true that he converted from Judaism to take up the post of musical director here in Vienna?"

"Sadly that's so. Anti-Semitism was at such a level that without his action he would never have been appointed, and so yes, he converted to Catholicism. But you have to remember that Vienna is the capital of music and such a position is the envy of every ambitious musician. However, I believe his real ambition is to be a composer, whilst his audience perceive him to be an outstanding conductor, with a habit of composing long symphonies. His time here has transformed the opera, which he's ruled like a dictator and, I have to admit, with wonderful results. I hope this gives him the inspiration to compose, which he seems to do in the summer months."

I could testify to his brilliant musical career as my mind raced ahead in time to the occasions I'd heard his symphonies, played in my home city in our outstanding Symphony Hall, by the City of Birmingham Symphony Orchestra, under the dynamic direction of Sir Simon Rattle.

Suddenly, the waiter arrived discreetly at the table, depositing the steaming drinks together with a large glass of cognac, which Herzl picked up quickly to take a couple of sips.

"And who is the young man sitting quietly at the table?"

"Ah let me think, I believe that's Arnold Schönberg. He's currently teaching in Berlin and it's rumored he'll soon move to Vienna. If I may add, this is the place for any radical musician with ambition to live."

I reflected on the young man Schönberg, as I studied him closely. He too had converted, but to Lutheranism, a few years earlier. It was to be another thirty years before he'd leave Berlin because his Jewish heritage couldn't be disguised, and return to his original faith. I noticed that the discussion was getting somewhat agitated at Mahler's table and I looked to Herzl for some explanation.

"I fear I can only share rumor and gossip," he said with a smile. "Strauss wishes to compose a piece based on Oscar Wilde's *Salome,* and Mahler is objecting. There's no way of knowing the outcome; we shall have to wait and see. But there's more to talk about and you'll be interested in my exploits. We've held three further Congresses, two in Basel and one in London, and have now decided to hold them every other year, so the next Congress, the sixth, will be next year. In Basel, we talked a great deal about the Jewish Colonial Trust and agreed that its funds would only be utilized in Palestine and, to a lesser extent, in Syria."

The Trust, about which he spoke, had been in existence for only a few years, having been conceived in 1897, although nothing definite happened until a year later. The intention was that it should become a commercial bank to purchase the land for settlement and this was achieved in 1899 when the bank was established in England, under English corporate law.

"And what about the London Congress – how significant was that?"

"Well, I suppose one of the significant aspects was the date, the beginning of the century, 1901. It was, however, overshadowed by concern among delegates for the plight of our people in Rumania. There was widespread anti-Semitism with thousands of Jews forced to leave their homes and others suffering persecution. This only added to the urgency of my goal and I was distressed not to be able to give more comfort to the Congress and the Jews of Rumania."

I could sense his frustration with the lack of progress as he continued to speak. "Last year in Basel, I was able to announce what I believed to be real progress. Vámbéry had kept his word although we paid him a high price, and I'd met with Sultan Abdul Hamid II in Constantinople. I can't remember the exact date, it was either May 17 or 18, and I was received at his Palace at Yildiz, just outside the city."

I really wanted to know more about this historical figure, a sultan and a caliph, titles which to me were recalled only in storybooks and theatrical pantomimes and who reigned over a mighty empire. "I want to know more about the sultan. What kind of man is he?"

"He doesn't travel extensively and whilst he cherishes many traditional values, some suggest that he's a great modernizer. He has a passion for photography and I was bemused when he requested a photograph of me before we met. I gather this is his custom when welcoming guests he doesn't know." We both smiled at this idiosyncrasy, as Herzl continued. "The sultan was dressed in a very impressive, albeit ill-fitting, uniform, covered in medals, quite short in height, rather thin and with a hooked nose and beard – not, I have to admit, a handsome figure. When I left I was mildly encouraged that he might support our wish for a charter, as he claimed to be a friend of the Jews, but I was disappointed when he told me that he'd only negotiate about land in Palestine after I'd delivered the loan in excess of £1 million. This was a great shock."

Herzl was obviously disappointed with this setback as he continued to relate his impressions of the 1901 Congress. "It was at this Congress that I met with some opposition led by three delegates, Motzkin, Weizmann and Buber."

The mention of Weizmann's name made me sit up. "Was this Chaim Weizmann?" I enquired, to be told that indeed it was. It would be impossible for me to share with Herzl the future of this young Zionist whose impact on Jewish history was to be immense, and who rose to become the first president of the State of Israel some half a century later.

"Am I correct in assuming that it was at this Congress when the Jewish National Fund was established?"

"Yes, I'm totally confident that the Jewish National Fund will become one of the foundations of the future of our people as they use the fund to build up a legacy which will provide the cash to buy and develop the land in Palestine. I have to admit to you that following this fifth Congress, I really felt a sense of achievement; that our goal was in sight, despite the opposition of the cultural Zionists."

"I can well understand what a stressful period you've had since we last met," I said quietly, as I was aware that he'd been unwell and that his father had died whilst he was in London, where he'd attempted to negotiate once more with Rothschild. I raised again the sensitive matter of the support of the great family.

"Let me tell you about the Rothschilds. For all my differences with the Baron Edmond de Rothschild – and I can only describe our relationship as strained and difficult – the family has been, without a doubt, the strongest supporter of Jewish immigration and settlement in Palestine. Edmond didn't go into the family banking business but chose to support art and culture. He, more than almost any other philanthropist, responded to the needs of his people following the pogroms in Russia and his generosity changed the lives and aspirations of thousands of Jews. He didn't only disagree with me," he added with a smile, "but with Ahad Ha'am too, and in that he was probably right."

I was fascinated by Herzl's acknowledgment of the efforts of Baron Edmond de Rothschild, especially as he had expressed so much disappointment in the support he'd received. He of course wouldn't know that Edmond died in Paris in 1934, having been appointed honorary president of the Jewish Agency, and twenty years later his remains, as well as those of his wife and cousin, the former Adelaide Rothschild, were brought to Ramat HaNadiv in Zichron Yaakov in Israel as their final resting place. His legacy was huge with the establishment of some thirty settlements and the reclamation of over 12,500 acres of land.

Herzl continued recounting about Rothschild. "Our initial meeting in 1896 was a disaster. I failed completely to convince him of our cause and I felt a sense of total frustration, as the atmosphere between us became full of animosity. I regret that, for he's a decent man who cares deeply about our people, and has demonstrated this in a tangible way not bettered by anyone else I know."

"Why do you think that you and Rothschild, who seemed to care so deeply about the Jewish people, couldn't agree on a common direction? Was it some form of arrogance or obstinacy?" I realized that my question was somewhat rude, but I was searching for an answer to this critical question which prevented two of the most visionary Jews of their time combining to bring about the establishment of a Jewish National Home. I couldn't help thinking that, if Herzl's dream could have come true at that time in history with the huge support which Rothschild could have given, maybe many millions of Jewish lives could have been saved from the Holocaust.

"I sense that we have different approaches to Zionism; mine is based on a practical cure for anti-Semitism, and as you will realize, without a religious foundation. Rothschild, however, seeks a state with a spiritual basis where Jews can live freely and at ease with their worship and tradition. Frankly, I think he feels that my efforts may well cause even more anti-Semitism. I wonder how history will judge us? Perhaps we're *both* wrong and have misjudged each other. We'll have to wait and see."

I felt a sense of great sorrow that the strong characters of these two men, both ardent Zionists, would somehow not allow them to work together, one harnessing the support of Jews and statesmen of the world, the other financing the early purchase of land and settlement of the pioneers. Who knows, perhaps the State of Israel, as we now know it, would have come about fifty years earlier and with less bloodshed and struggle.

"Three months ago I met with Lord Nathaniel Mayer Rothschild in London. Sadly this meeting followed my being recalled to Vienna by Julie, because my father was desperately ill, and as you know he died in June."

As we finished our drinks the conversation turned away from Zionism and the Holy Land to other world affairs. "I was saddened to hear of the death of Cecil Rhodes in March, for it was his Charter for South Africa which attracted me as an example of what we might achieve for Palestine. On the happier side, it's good to see that the Boer War has ended. Our newspapers covered Kitchener's triumphant return to England…and now, Zissman, what of your new King, how is he being received?"

"I believe quite well, but Edward VII will find it very hard to follow his mother, Queen Victoria, whose death last year left the country in deep sorrow. The funeral was an international event and even the kaiser, Wilhelm II, attended."

"I would have expected no less, after all he's Victoria's grandson. But what is this I hear about Joseph Chamberlain's anti-German speech which seems to have caused so much trouble?"

"Well, I notice that von Bülow responded in equally aggressive terms." My reply brought a wry smile from Herzl, who commented, "It's sad that Anglo-German relations have sunk so low. It's rumored that the kaiser himself is considering a visit to England to repair the damage, but I suspect it'll be some months before that happens."

"Speaking of Mr. Chamberlain, our colonial secretary, I've heard reports that you've met with him and you'll be aware of our mutual connection with the city of Birmingham."

"Indeed I am, because I came to meet with him through the good offices of Mr. Leopold Greenberg, who spent time with Chamberlain in Birmingham, when both were members of the Liberal Party there."

Joseph Chamberlain was of course an icon in the life of Birmingham. He was the father of Neville – who became the British prime minister who had the fateful meeting in 1938 with Adolf Hitler at his German retreat. – Joseph Chamberlain was one of the great municipal leaders in local government. He had shown outstanding vision in developing the city with ambitious civic schemes and enterprise bringing into public ownership the various utilities, such as water and gas. Having been elected to the House of Commons as a Member of Parliament for Birmingham, as well as moving between the Liberal and Conservative Parties, he was described as the most powerful man in British politics. It is this man who set an example for generations of city councillors who followed him, not least of all me, culminating in my serving as the city's lord mayor a century after Chamberlain himself.

Herzl didn't appear to notice my temporary loss of attention as he continued to speak. "Greenberg attended our last Zionist Congress and reported some significant news about Jewish immigration to England. He claimed that over the last decade or so the numbers have increased by 25,000 and this has caused concern among the public, who regarded these people as cheap labor and a threat to the host population."

"Wasn't this one of the forces behind the Royal Commission established in London to consider controls on immigration?"

"Yes, the Commission which met last July was charged with examining the extent of alien immigration into Britain, and what measures might be needed to restrict what is seen as a lack of border controls. This is particularly so compared with the United States of America, which is adopting quite severe checks on those seeking to enter the country. Jewish immigration is of particular concern, as many of those fleeing from oppression in Eastern Europe took up work in the East End of London, in tailoring and the furniture trade and other industries where conditions were poor and in which the local population simply won't work."

I listened to this with some disbelief as I realized that history does indeed repeat itself, for within the century that followed our conversation, exactly the same words were being heard in Britain again, this time about the new waves of immigration from Eastern Europe, the Asian subcontinent and the West Indies.

"What was the agenda for your meeting with Chamberlain and how did he react to your vision for Palestine, considering Britain's own ambitions for its Empire?"

"I met him only a week or so ago, so the meeting is fresh in my mind. First of all we discussed the Royal Commission, which I'd attended, and he asked for my impressions. I recognized the privilege of meeting a member of the British government and, wanting to be courteous, asked him first of all if he had recovered from his accident, because I heard he'd suffered a fall.

"He shrugged his shoulders as if dismissing my inquiry, so I continued. I said that I'd tried to explain to the Commission that Jews came to England because they sought freedom for their life, as well as their belief, but on arrival still found themselves as aliens. My next statement may well have struck a chord with one of the panel, Lord Rothschild, as I ventured to suggest that Jews were often themselves the cause of the anti-Semitism they wished to defeat."

"Did you suggest an answer to this situation?" I inquired.

"Absolutely, and that was the establishment of a state where they would be recognized as being in their own national home. But I also took the opportunity to make him aware that whilst the European leaders were bringing pressure on the Ottomans to allow more land in Palestine to be purchased by Jews, the reverse was in fact taking place as Zionist immigration was being restricted and land acquisition around the city of Jerusalem curtailed. Mr. Chamberlain showed understanding of my argument and took out of his drawer a copy of my plans which I'd sent to him via Lord Rothschild. Our conversation moved away from Palestine as we mentioned alternative locations, including Cyprus and El-Arish. He seemed familiar with the former as this area came under his jurisdiction as minister for the colonies, but mention of El-Arish caused a blank expression and I realized he was unsure where this was. He took me to a wall map and I pointed to the Sinai in Egypt where El-Arish sat in the northern sector."

I expressed some surprise at Chamberlain's lack of awareness about where El-Arish was, because having built a successful business in Birmingham which traded worldwide, he'd been an inveterate traveler.

"Chamberlain then explained that whilst he may have some influence in Cyprus, he'd have to refer me to his cabinet colleague, Lord Lansdowne, who was the foreign secretary and responsible for relations with Egypt."

"And how long did it take to arrange this meeting?" I asked, suspecting that the government bureaucracy would cause a long delay.

"You'll be surprised to know that I saw him almost immediately, and he agreed to make contact with Lord Cromer, the consul general who effectively controlled Egypt. He was certainly a man of action, because he suggested that he dispatch Mr. Greenberg to meet with Lord Cromer to discuss the proposal."

"I can sense your enthusiasm for this idea, so we'll await the outcome with interest."

We'd been sitting and talking nonstop for some time and Herzl summoned a waiter to replenish our drinks. I never needed a second invitation to taste the delights of the Sacher Hotel.

"It appears, Dr. Herzl, that you've mixed with the great and the good of our country, and gained audiences which can only be due to your persistence and character. What's your current impression of the progress you're making?"

"An interesting question, and as I've said to you before, it's always a mix of success and disappointment. One of the things which has caused me great concern is the attitude of what I shall call the Jewish assimilated establishment and the Jewish leadership which sadly includes Chief Rabbi Hermann Adler. I've had more support and encouragement from the British Government, even kind, if not guarded, words from Lord Salisbury, your prime minister and Mr. Gladstone, who wrote to Sir Samuel Montagu expressing a view about what he called an 'interesting idea.'"

"I'm not surprised to hear what you say about the Jewish establishment; they tend to feel that they're more English than Jewish and don't want to give up what they've won."

"Maybe, but thinking that they're isolated from the anti-Semitism sweeping through Europe is unwise. What's become clear to me is the gulf which has opened up between the Jews of the East End, mostly immigrants, and the 'better off' who live in the more affluent suburbs of London. It's as if we have two distinct Jewish communities."

I couldn't help speculating whether even the passing of 100 years would change all of this in the sprawling metropolis of London, where success had come to some families, but not to all. "You speak of the support of the Government. How much of this is due, do you think, to self-interest?"

"A perceptive question, and you're right. The English are anxious to solve the problem of cheap labor, predominantly in the East End, but they also have another agenda, and that's to curb the influence of Ottoman power in the Middle East. But for all of that, I love your fine country, ever since my first visit over thirteen years ago to the Isle of Wight and Brighton. I admire its sense of history and freedom. I see the role of Empire builder as an example of global development, and I've no doubt that given time it will be the British Government which makes the commitment to a Jewish National Home, hopefully in Palestine."

With these prophetic words, I finished my chocolate, Herzl his cognac, and we took our leave. I wasn't sure when we'd next meet.

CHAPTER ELEVEN

Rome, Italy, 1904

1903 had come and gone, another interesting year in the birth of a new century, which would bring so much sadness to the world and unforgettable horror for the Jewish people. A period which would contain two World Wars, with millions of innocent victims.

In the United States there was concern that the number of immigrants entering the country each year had reached one million, some seventy percent from Eastern Europe, compared with just seven percent thirty years earlier. Most were either Catholics or Jews, and the usual questions were being asked by the trade unions about the challenge to jobs of the host population. It seems to me so strange that this question is always asked and inevitably from those who are themselves descendants of immigrants. I couldn't help but hope that Henry Ford's new business would employ many of these new workers, as I was convinced they'd have the skills to build motor cars.

History continued to be made. Wilbur and Orville Wright, after so many abortive attempts, made their first flight. Madame Curie became the first woman to be awarded the Nobel Prize for physics, alongside her husband. And there were rumblings of war between Japan and Russia. There was a hunger for exploration, particularly to the Antarctic with Captain Robert Scott and Ernest Shackleton amongst the first to venture south, albeit unsuccessfully.

Life for the five million Jews in Russia was becoming hard again with a pogrom in Kishenev, starting on Easter morning. Under the oppressive reign of Czar Nicholas II, the police turned a blind eye to the murder, rape and injury of some 500 Jews, as well as the destruction of over 1,500 shops and homes by frenzied peasants. And this was only the beginning, as the troubles spread to Kiev and Odessa, stirred up by student factions. Jews were forbidden by government decree to own property outside of areas in which they resided and, not surprisingly, objections by the American government were swept aside.

Further east, there were earthquakes in Jerusalem and Constantinople, and the great railway development was under way with new lines being built from Berlin to Baghdad, as well as to Constantinople. Back in England, politics was making news. Joseph Chamberlain was having huge problems with his parliamentary colleagues over his plans to introduce tariffs to protect the British colonies. Eventually in September 1903, he resigned from the government, although the family continued to hold high office when a month later, Joseph's son, Austen, was appointed chancellor of the exchequer. Four times Conservative prime minister, Lord Salisbury, who had retired as premier in 1902, died and was succeeded by his nephew, Arthur Balfour, who was destined to play such a major part in the future of the Zionist dream. Britain was beginning to feel the influence of Emily Pankhurst in her drive to obtain votes for women.

1904 had begun with the Russo-Japanese War which had started because both countries had imperialistic ambitions in Korea and Manchuria. It was against this tapestry of the period that the scene for my next meeting with Herzl, in Italy, was set. I was sitting in the lounge of the Quirinale Hotel on Rome's Via Nazionale, waiting for Herzl to join me for breakfast, on what was a cold and crisp January morning. My elegant bedroom at the rear of the hotel overlooked the Opera House and I could hear the strains of the music and singing even through the closed shutters. My thoughts were interrupted as Herzl appeared at the door and I rose to meet him and take our seats in the dining room. He looked tired and confirmed this with his opening words, "Good morning. I trust your night was better than mine."

I had to admit that I'd slept well, as I always felt comfortable under a European-style quilt, something we in England only became accustomed to in later years. We had met briefly the previous evening on my arrival, and I was eagerly looking forward to our breakfast, when I'd been promised an update on his travels and meetings.

"Last year has probably been one of the most arduous so far," he started, "visits starting in January to London to meet with Chamberlain and Rothschild, to Paris for meetings with Nordau and Marmorek, and then to Cairo for discussions with Lord Cromer and Boutros Ghali. In August I made an interesting visit to St. Petersburg, meeting government leaders as well as some of our own people. I don't appear to have had even a day's rest other than a couple of brief stays at Edlach – set in the Austrian mountains where I found a peaceful and restful environment, as I also went to Konstanz in Germany to discuss my dilemma with Friedrich of Baden. Of course, I was also traveling backwards and forwards to Vienna, not to mention the Sixth Congress in Basel."

One couldn't help but be amazed at the energy of this man, who was clearly not in the best of health and looking extremely tired from his travels and testing negotiations.

"What of the last Congress? How significant was the offer of the British Government, and what is the latest position – as I know you have placed so much faith in their support? Now that Chamberlain has resigned, are you still being well received?"

There was a pause, whilst some coffee was poured, and a silver dish of breads and pastries was placed before us.

"Chamberlain's resignation was a disappointment. He'd been in Africa early in 1903 and had identified what he felt would be an ideal tract of land for Jewish settlement. It was in Paris that I discussed our reply with Nordau and Greenberg."

I was surprised by this revelation as I understood that Herzl's sole objective, supported by the Zionist movement, was that Palestine was the only location acceptable and I shared this view with him.

"What was their reply, because I was always under the impression that there was only one option for the Jewish State?"

"That's certainly true for many of our political Zionists, but I had to face reality. Despite sending a commission to Cairo with some distinguished members to examine the feasibility of El-Arish, Lord Cromer, the British government's man in Egypt, has set his mind against any Jewish settlement. This was supported by the Egyptian foreign minister, Butros Ghali, even though my good friend Greenberg had also been in Cairo for a couple of months negotiating on my behalf. As for the Congress, I called on the delegates to give serious consideration to the Uganda option, which the British had formalized just days before we met. You can imagine that the debate was, let's say, lively. Nordau was a great supporter, putting forward a view that perhaps this might be a short-term measure, and despite this passionate appeal, nearly 100 abstained. Sadly, this was strange as I felt the urgency of moving Jews away from the anti-Semitism in Eastern Europe justified the proposal. "

"You received a report from Greenberg, didn't you?"

"I did," came the sharp reply, "and I began to speculate how good a friend he was when he confirmed that a charter would certainly not be granted. He had avoided me, which made me feel uncomfortable. His report was inconclusive and it seemed to me a poor result. I decided that I must go myself and meet with Lord Cromer and the commission, and suggest some compromise about the charter. That's why I speak of *reality*. Chamberlain had been touring South and East Africa following the end of the Boer War, and spotted some land along the railway line from Nairobi, the capital of British East Africa, referred to as Uganda, and apparently empty of people. Chamberlain thought this ideal for the Jewish Home and he asked to see me. When such a proposal comes from a member of the British government, it's surely worthy of consideration."

I thought about this as he spoke and speculated that the location identified by Chamberlain was actually Kenya, and known as the Uasin Gishu Plateau, named for the Masai tribe who were not identified with Uganda.

"What was so special about the idea? Perhaps it was Chamberlain's view that this was the better of all evils as he didn't wish to upset the Arabs or the Turks by pursuing the Palestine option?" I didn't add my personal thoughts about the traditional and longstanding pro-Arab bias held by the Foreign Office in England.

"That may well be one motive; another may have been the wish to rid London of cheap labor and solving what's become known as 'the Jewish problem.'"

"Chamberlain was the colonial secretary and I suspect that originally he was influenced by a settlement of Jews in Sinai or that region as being an effective extension of British colonial power," I suggested.

Herzl nodded, without too much conviction, as he continued, "but he also thought the climate would suit us, even those coming from Europe. The land was ideal for growing cotton and sugar with adequate irrigation, something lacking in El-Arish as the Egyptians simply couldn't spare water from the Nile."

I could sense Herzl's continuing frustration. "It seems to me that this Uganda plan was always going to be difficult to sell to your supporters, particularly those in Russia."

"Yes, but I was encouraged when I traveled to St. Petersburg and Vilna last August. It was a most exhilarating visit." His response seemed to revive him, as he explained the success of the visit. "I was asking for some intervention from the Russian government with the sultan to allow Jewish settlement and just as important for a more liberal attitude to Zionist activity. But the happiest aspects of my journey were a banquet with the Zionists in St. Petersburg and, a few days later, a wonderful reception in Vilna."

Mention of Vilna sparked memories of my own ancestors' early life in Biala Podlaska in Russian Poland, and I was determined to discuss this with Herzl when the opportunity presented itself.

"I must admit that the welcome afforded me in Vilna was good for both the spirit and the soul," said Herzl with a wry smile, "they were overly generous in their words, and as we drove through the streets of the Jewish quarter, I was amazed at the impact of my visit. It was difficult to shield the tears when I considered the utter despair of these poor people as they lived under such a repressive regime."

I didn't want to interrupt him as he thought for a moment before adding, "If it were for no other reason, then our mission and dream to build a permanent home for the Jewish people was justified by the plight of the Jews of Russia."

Our breakfast had come to a close and Herzl went off to prepare for his meeting with King Vittorio Emanuele III. The previous day, January 22, he'd met with the papal secretary, Rafael Merry del Val, and had secured a pledge of qualified support. I was amazed when he told me that later that week he was to be received by Pope Pius X himself, a singular honor for anyone, but for a Jew a spectacular honor. This was a man who would be canonized half a century later, and I reflected briefly on Herzl's desire ten years earlier to ask the pope to convert the Jews, as an option which might cure anti-Semitism. This time his mission was a very different one.

I decided to spend a few days touring Rome and its environs and hoped that I would meet with Herzl before he left Italy, to hear about his meeting at the Vatican, an assurance he was generous enough to give.

I was waiting in the lounge of the hotel when Herzl returned from his visit and he was as good as his word. His face appeared to show that he'd been poorly received. I called for a couple of drinks as he slumped into an armchair looking tired and dejected. I said nothing, waiting for him to speak.

"Perhaps I had too much of an expectation from someone who'd been appointed barely a few months earlier." He shrugged his shoulders, "the pope was standing when Dr. Lippe and I arrived. He was dressed in his white papal robes, with matching skullcap and pure white hair, and his kindly face disguised his approaching seventieth birthday. He extended his hand for the traditional kiss, which I didn't give, although I'd been advised that this was expected, but Lippe knelt and kissed his hand. I suspect this might have been a bad start to the meeting, but this wasn't so. The Holy Father, however, made his position very clear. He wouldn't support the return of the Jews to Palestine and he expressed his total opposition to us ever having control of Jerusalem, although he had no objection to Jews living there. I felt that the divide between the Catholics and the Jews had widened, despite my attempts to speak kindly and with a degree of respect and conciliation. He said that as Jews had never recognized Jesus and still awaited the Messiah, he couldn't recognize the Jews."

That night, I doubt either of us slept well. I was kept awake thinking of a visit to Israel nearly 100 years later in March 2000 by Pope John Paul II. President Ezer Weizman in his welcome had said, "There is a question whether history makes a leader, or a leader makes history. You, Your Holiness, without doubt, clearly leave your mark and influence on history and through your character, your conduct, and your personal influence, unites the hearts of humanity." Attitudes change over the generations, summed up by the words of Pope John Paul II when he visited the Rome Synagogue in 1986, "with Judaism, we have a relationship that we do not have with other religions. You are our dearly beloved brothers; in a certain way, indeed, it could be said that you are our elder brothers."

As our stay in Rome came to an end, I was to return to Birmingham, and Herzl to Vienna.

CHAPTER TWELVE

Edlach, Austria, 1904

News reached me around the time of Easter and Passover 1904 that Herzl had been taken ill, and that his doctors had ordered him to rest at Franzensbad in Austria. I was distressed because I wanted to continue my conversations with him. When we'd last met in Rome, he'd appeared very tired, which showed not just in his face but in his whole body.

Despite his failing health he wasn't prepared to give up the effort to reach his goal, the search for support to establish a home for the Jewish people. During the early months of the year he continued to be in contact with Leopold Greenberg, who was strongly recommending that he accept the offer of the British government of a piece of "ideal" land in East Africa, particularly as there was a probability of a change of government and the option might possibly disappear. He was still attempting to negotiate with the Ottoman government over land in Palestine, and making renewed approaches to the Russian minister of the interior, Vyacheslav von Plehve, even though the Russians had their hands full with the war with Japan as well as open rebellion at home. Herzl finally met von Plehve in St. Petersburg in 1903. It was a strange choice for support in view of his reputation for being cruel, as well as anti-Semitic. Indeed, it was even suggested that von Plehve was behind the pogroms against the Jews. He was a repeated target for assassination, which finally succeeded some three weeks after Herzl himself died.

Just days before he was taken ill, he was planning further visits to Paris and London to follow up the meeting he'd convened in April of the Greater Actions Committee of the Zionist Movement. He told me that at that meeting his aim was to bring together the different factions of the Zionist movement who were divided between the short-term remedy of Uganda and the long-term vision of Palestine. Herzl's skill had resulted in fresh unity. His follow-up meetings were to try and secure funding for an expedition to Uganda. He now had a new target in his sights as he made contact with Jacob Schiff, a wealthy and powerful American Jew. Herzl hoped Schiff might finance a loan to the Russians in return for some compassion for the Jews living there, even though he'd made it clear that he thought Herzl's ideas no more than a sentimental dream.

Herzl's doctor, Katzenelson, visited him at Franzensbad and, having consulted other physicians, knew that he had a life-threatening heart condition but was unsure of the exact nature of the cause and the treatment required. Herzl returned to Vienna but within weeks was again taken ill, and was moved to Edlach. It was here, in late June, that I was privileged to meet with him for a short time.

I was welcomed by Julie, his wife, whose haggard look clearly showed both her concern and the silent plea that I shouldn't stay long. She offered me a cup of hot chocolate and showed me into his room, where he was sitting quietly by the window, reading a newspaper. He looked up, smiled and extended his hand. I was immediately shocked by his condition – he was, after all, only forty-four years old, but he appeared short of breath, somehow drained and suffering pain. But he was by no means finished.

"Sit, my friend. Thank you for coming. I'm delighted to see you. I want to share with you some private thoughts." He sat for a few moments without speaking, perhaps thinking whether the admission he was about to make was appropriate. "I'm ill and have been troubled about my son, Hans. Last month, he reached the age of bar mitzva and, because he'd never been circumcised, he couldn't undertake the traditional synagogue ceremony. What have I achieved if I've not been a good father and husband?"

This was a question to which I felt totally incapable of offering a reasonable answer. I was only too well aware of the dangers of public life and the shift of priorities which often threatened parental responsibility. I wanted, however, to return our conversation to the cause to which he'd dedicated himself over the last twenty years.

"I'm sure that with medical care and the support of your wife and family your strength will return, as you still have much to do if the Jewish people are to have their own state."

"Maybe, but I suspect that the hours are draining away, and that it'll be left to others to complete what I've started." He picked up a piece of paper and handed it to me. It was written in his own handwriting. "This document has never been made public and I wrote it on a previous visit to Edlach. I had discussed its contents with some close friends at the last Basel Congress – good friends, Nordau, Zangwill and Joseph Cowen, who, you will be interested to learn, is a Jew and an English businessman. It is a letter to the Jewish people."

I looked at the document, written in German, which I couldn't understand. I said quietly, "Could you please read it to me?"

He nodded. "I'll give you the meaning of the letter." He paused as he took back the letter, and stared at it for a moment or two, before continuing. "We've come to the parting of the ways and it is the personality of the leader which determines the future path. I wanted to put on record my disappointment that had I been listened to in 1901 then the Jews might well have acquired Palestine. Because our people did not will it, it remains a dream from which we'll awaken in the future. We're a divided people and should a split come, then my *heart* remains with the Zionists and my *reason* with those seeking to settle in East Africa. I cannot with all honesty continue to lead the movement so long as there is conflict and I'll withdraw with dignity, and without any bitterness. No one, even my enemies – and of course I have made some along the journey – can accuse me of making any material gain from our movement, and I'm therefore content to put up with the attacks which have been made upon me. And yet I've been rewarded by my people with their love and respect. They're a good people and yet an unhappy people and I pray God will help them achieve happiness and a home."

This explanation seemed to drain him and although he was smiling slightly I could sense the deep disappointment that, despite all his effort, his travels, his diplomacy and his total commitment, he'd been unable to achieve his one goal in life, the establishment of a national home for the Jewish people.

"I sense a feeling of disappointment, but there's still time. Jews are not always the fastest people to make a decision, certainly the right decision."

Herzl smiled and gently shook his head. "My time's passing. I'm tired, and it's for others to take over where I've left off. When I look at you, I have a message to give and it is that I charge you, Bernard Zissman, and your generation, to complete the task I've started. I remember once telling my children as I reflected on my own childhood watching my father light the traditional lights on the Hanukkah menorah, 'a nation is born at Hanukkah, the first and lonely candle cannot defeat the darkness, and little by little as the eight candles are lit, the darkness recedes and a sense of satisfaction arrives as the task is complete.' So I've lit the first candle and it's time for others to take on the mantle – light the other candles and finish the work."

I sat transfixed by the words of this man who had devoted his short but full life for the benefit of his people. I recalled how it had all begun, the influence on Herzl of the evil of anti-Semitism, first in Vienna, later in Paris, and then seeing it spread across Europe. Some Zionists appeared to accept anti-Semitism as inevitable, to be cured only by having their own land; some saw the aim of a Jewish state as an answer to a renewal of Judaism. Some never accept, and continue to deny the existence of anti-Semitism, and believe that assimilation is the answer to a society which preserves this evil via racism of all kinds and against all minorities.

Julie Herzl had entered the room as if to give a signal that it was time for me to leave. I rose and took both of Herzl's hands in mine, as I bade him farewell and thanked him for the usual generosity of his time. He struggled to rise from his chair and waved aside my objections. I felt there was some finality in our parting words as I wished him well and left the room.

In the hallway Julie had been joined by her daughter, Pauline. I turned to Julie, looking unwell herself, to thank her for the kind hospitality. Her eyes filled with tears and she coughed quietly as she spoke. "He has a severe bout of bronchitis and there's a danger that it'll turn to pneumonia. We've summoned the doctors and are considering how to tell his mother, who's unaware of his condition. She'll be shocked but I know that Theodor will want to see her, should his condition seriously worsen. Reverend Hechler, who is a dear friend, is also planning a visit and we expect our two younger children, Hans and Trudi, to accompany their grandmother."

On Sunday July 3, 1904, at five o'clock in the afternoon, Theodor Herzl died at Edlach. I couldn't help but speculate whether he died of a weak heart or a *broken* heart.

*   *   *

I decided to travel to Döblinger Friedhof in Vienna a few days later to witness his funeral. The service was held at ten o'clock in the morning in the library at Herzl's home; the coffin was covered by the blue and white Zionist flag, and rested on trestles with a single floral tribute. It was a simple service, as required by Jewish law, and even though I found the presence of many bouquets somewhat foreign to Jewish custom, I was deeply moved by the strong voices of the cantors and choir singing out loudly the haunting melodies of the funeral service. The service concluded with Herzl's son, Hans, reciting in Hebrew the *Kaddish*, the prayer for the dead. Before everyone left the library for the final resting place, Herzl's friend and supporter, David Wolffsohn, turned to face those present and raising his right arm in a gesture inviting them to join him began to recite the words from Psalm 137, which Herzl had used to conclude the Sixth Zionist Congress, "If I forget thee, O Jerusalem, may my right hand wither."

The assembly consisted of a catalogue of Zionist leaders and I couldn't help but gasp as I recognized the giants of Jewish history – Stefan Zweig, the Austrian writer; Arthur Schnitzler, not a confirmed Zionist but admirer of Herzl; Martin Buber, a cultural Zionist; and, naturally, Herzl's great friend, Max Nordau.

Following this, everyone moved in total silence towards the place of burial, the vault in which Herzl's father had been laid to rest just two years earlier, and where Theodor Herzl would lie until his remains were re-interred forty-five years later on Mount Herzl in the city of his dreams, Jerusalem. I stood some distance from the graveside looking at the surrounding hills of Vienna and watched as thousands of mourners – estimates say 6,000 – dressed in a range of traditional clothes reflecting their home countries, from England to France, Germany and Austria and across the rest of the European continent, gathered to bid farewell to this unique leader of the Jewish people.

News of his death passed speedily around the Jewish world and was greeted with shock and grief, even though stories of his illness were well known. In Eastern Europe, feelings were especially emotive, as Herzl was seen by the masses as their savior from oppression and persecution. Many went to their local synagogue to say prayers and, as has always been the custom among Jews, to congregate to share their grief and sorrow.

I left Vienna, my head full of thoughts about the experience of meeting this great man and wondering what the future would bring his family. It was already clear to most around him that Herzl's life had been dominated by his commitment to what he had called his "dream", the establishment of a Jewish national home in Palestine. He had neglected his profession and the opportunity to use his considerable writing and journalistic skills to live a comfortable life, choosing instead to use his own resources to fund the travel and everything else needed to race around Europe in search of support for his idea. Whilst he had told Rev. Hechler as he lay dying, "Tell them that I've given my heart's blood for my people," he'd also given of his worldly possessions and died penniless.

In the brief conversations I'd shared with Julie Herzl, she confided that she'd not publicly supported her husband's efforts and had feared that giving his life to the dream which had all but consumed him would end unhappily. And in her own words, captured in *Die Welt*, she quietly and, I thought, proudly, admitted, "I will serve the Zionist movement as long as I'm able. I'll encourage my children to do so too and hopefully they'll carry on and be worthy successors to their father. His dream will one day become a reality and I can only express my love for him through our efforts to continue what he's started."

Sadly none of this was to come about. Julie's health, which had not been good for some time, declined very quickly after her husband's death. Following spells in various nursing homes, she died in 1907, at Bad Aussee, at the early age of just thirty-nine, and was outlived by her mother-in-law who died four years later. She had decreed that she wished her body to be wiped out entirely and as a result, she was cremated, in contravention of strict Jewish law.

This was not to be the end of the Herzl family saga, which moved from one tragedy to another. Theodor and Julie's son, Hans, was circumcised after his mother's death, moved to England, became naturalized and underwent conversion to Christianity, although he didn't seem to make a long-term commitment, returning eventually to Liberal Judaism. He lived in poverty, despite being educated at Clifton College and obtaining a scholarship to Cambridge, and eventually committed suicide in 1930. His sister Pauline, who had suffered from various psychiatric illnesses and an unsuccessful marriage, died from drug addiction in the same year. There's a suggestion that the effect of his sister's death drove

Hans to shoot himself. Both were buried at Bordeaux in a Jewish cemetery, and it was to be more than seventy years before the bodies were re-interred on Mount Herzl, finally respecting one of Herzl's dying wishes.

Herzl's third child, Trudi, was declared insane, and although she lived longer than her brother and sister, she had an equally unhappy and tragic life. Together with her husband, she was deported in 1942 by the Nazis to the Theresienstadt concentration camp and died a year later. Trudi had one son, Stefan Neumann, who served as an officer in the British army, visited Palestine, and settled in Washington as a diplomat in the British Embassy. As if to confirm that at a curse had been cast on the Herzl family, he committed suicide in 1946.

When I reflected on the legacy Theodor Herzl had bequeathed, I felt a deep sadness. History is full of great personalities whose influence and impact have changed the direction of the world, but whose failure to build a happy family heritage seems to have escaped them. Herzl was no different. He has motivated generations of Jews that followed him, people like me and so many others, and perhaps we have lessons to learn about how we live our lives and create a balance between the love of our families and the love of our people.

1. Herzl's final resting place in Jerusalem

2. Herzl aged 26 in 1886

3. Herzl aged 39 in 1899

4. Herzl's study in Vienna

122B

5. Julie Herzl

6. Herzl with his mother
and British friends: (left
to right) J.L. Greenberg,
I. Zangwill, Col. Goldsmid

*7. The famous photo of Herzl on the balcony
of the Drei Könige Hotel in Basel*

8. Herzl greeting the kaiser at Mikve Yisrael

9. Zionist delegation to Jerusalem in 1898, including David Wolffsohn (second left) and Herzl (center)

10. At the Fifth Zionist Congress in Basel in 1902, with Herzl in the center of the second row and Chaim Weizmann second row first left

11. Herzl leaving the Basel Synagogue in 1903

12. Herzl's funeral in Vienna in 1904

13. Herzl's grave in Vienna

14. Zionist Commission to Palestine in 1917, with Chaim Weizmann (forefront) and Lord Samuel (in uniform)

PART TWO
THE REALITY

CHAPTER THIRTEEN

Vienna, Austria, 2005

It was December 2005, and I found myself once again in Vienna. It was cold, the sun was shining brightly, and the streets were crowded. I made my way down the Graben with its shops and musical entertainers of immense quality and talent, either amateurs or "resting" professionals. In Stephansplatz I looked up at St. Stephen's Cathedral, dominating the entire square and beyond, surrounded by scaffolding and drapes shielding the never-ending refurbishment. I turned to walk slowly down Kärntner Strasse. I was heading for the Sacher Hotel, an Austrian institution, where I once sat drinking coffee in 1890 having that memorable meeting with Herzl. I stood by the entrance. I glanced around and wondered what the Viennese of either the last or the present century, the inventors of the coffee house, would think of the arrival of Starbucks opposite the traditional Sacher Coffee House. There appeared no queue over that side of the street.

I stood patiently for a little time reflecting on my visit, when I'd visited the great Opera House and saw *La Traviata*, and earlier in the day, pushing my way up the congested steps of the Historisches Museum to visit the stunning Goya Exhibition.

I decided that I wouldn't wait in a queue moving so slowly, so I made my way around the corner and through the main entrance of the hotel in Philharmonikerstrasse, to a quieter lounge near the elegant dining room. Beautiful chandeliers hung from the high ceilings, heavy drapes covered the windows and portraits hung everywhere. I recalled my earlier visit and was struck by the thought that some things in life simply don't change. This wasn't the case in the street scene. Gone were the bicycles and the streetcars, and in their place was a pedestrian area filled with elegant couples, many of the ladies dressed warmly in fur coats and fashionable boots. In many ways it didn't seem a far cry from the days a century ago when men in dark dress coats, accompanied by elegant ladies in designer hats and beautiful dresses, strolled casually through the main streets. In 2005 the city was throbbing with tourists. December was high season as visitors from every country of the world appeared to be taking pictures.

I settled down in a comfortable armchair and closed my eyes as my mind drifted back over a century to the time of Gustav Mahler, Sigmund Freud, Arnold Schönberg (who had anglicized his name when he left Germany and re-converted to Judaism) and Stefan Zweig, who had so influenced the thinking and music not just of this city but of a whole generation – at a time when Vienna had been at the forefront of anti-Semitism. The stories of these great composers, authors and thinkers, all of whom, despite in some cases converting to Christianity, were the targets of anti-Semitism, the Nazis and Hitler. Even Richard Strauss, a non-Jew, Austrian through and through, and composer of the Olympic Hymn for the 1936 Berlin games, didn't escape the wrath of the Nazis, because he had a Jewish daughter-in-law and had worked with Zweig.

Above all there was Theodor Herzl, a giant of his day and a man destined to change the course of Jewish history. I suppose l slipped into a quiet drowse and might have stayed that way if a sudden movement hadn't disturbed me.

I opened my eyes slowly and then closed them again to make sure I wasn't in a dream, before opening them wide to look at the man who sat in a chair opposite me. There was no mistaking the image of Theodor Herzl, his formal coat, his shiny silk top hat resting on the striped trousers and his shock of black hair and distinguished beard.

I sat for a moment or two staring at him before murmuring quietly, "Is it you, Dr. Herzl?"

"Yes, it is. Welcome to Vienna. It is indeed many years since we last met, much has happened in this world of ours and I'm anxious to hear from you; how life has changed and the results, if any, of all of my efforts a hundred years ago."

"I'm not sure how to start, for the world has moved in many directions, not all of the journeys being happy ones, especially for the Jewish people."

"Well, I challenge you to make an effort. I want to know about our people, about Palestine, what of the struggles in Europe and, if I may ask, what of you? You know of my lifetime's commitment to Zionism. Tell me about *your* commitment and those of your generation – indeed if you have a commitment at all. I have time, plenty of it, so begin when you choose and let's dream together." He paused, and then spoke.

"And, my friend, as we've spent so much time together, perhaps we should introduce some informality. Please call me Theodor and I'll respond likewise, if this is agreeable."

CHAPTER FOURTEEN

Birmingham, England, 1945

I am not sure when I first became a Zionist. Maybe I was born one, or just grew into one. *I know that I'll die one.*

My family was traditionally Jewish, and like my father before me, I was born in Birmingham, in the heart of England. My paternal grandfather had come to the city in 1906 from the East End of London, then the home of many Jewish refugees fleeing from the pogroms of Europe and deeply felt anti-Semitism throughout Eastern Europe, well before the Nazis came to power.

So what was traditional Judaism in 1930s England and particularly in Birmingham, a city of over a million people, some 100 miles northwest of London? The city was the hub of the nation's manufacturing strength. Within its boundaries you would find factories of every conceivable size and style. At the heart of the city was the jewelry quarter and home to small manufacturing businesses designing and making some of the finest jewelry and silverware to be found anywhere in the world, leading to Birmingham earning the title "city of a thousand trades".

Further out of the city were the garden factory of the Cadbury family, churning out mountains of milk chocolate, and Austin's motor car plant. Here was one of the bases of Birmingham's industrial heritage as the Austin ranked alongside some of the greatest auto brands ever known. The streets were full of ranges of cars bearing the names Wolseley, Sunbeam Talbot and Hillman, whilst those with more money to spend drove around in Rovers and Jaguars.

It was within this environment that I was born at the end of 1934. Europe was alive to talk of the rise in National Socialism in Germany, where Hitler's Nazis had become the largest party in the Reichstag, gaining 13 million new voters a year earlier. Germany's President von Hindenburg had appointed Hitler as Chancellor, the Third Reich had been announced, and life for Jews was becoming more and more difficult by the month, if not the day. Within the twelve months prior to my birth, kosher meat had been banned in Germany, Jewish shops were boycotted, marriage to Jews was forbidden and Jewish teachers were dismissed from their positions. No one was exempt. An edict was issued that all doctors must be members of the Nazi Party. Even the eminent scientist Albert Einstein had his bank account seized, and outstanding conductors Erich Kleiber and Otto Klemperer fled for their lives. Following the fire at the previous Reichstag, a new building was opened where representation was decreed to be Nazi only. No Jews or women were permitted. Dachau, the first of the infamous concentration camps, had been established near Munich, and by the beginning of 1934 already housed 5,000 political prisoners.

In Palestine, German immigrants were anxious to secure a new home, and they established a settlement at Nahariya in the north, close to the Lebanese border. David Ben-Gurion, later to become Israel's first prime minister, was inspired to explore the opportunities he found in the southern desert of the Negev. He demonstrated considerable vision by traveling to meet with Arab leaders, proposing a Jewish state alongside an independent Palestinian Arab state. It was in this year that the seeds of anger were planted with the British authorities. They feared problems with the Arabs over Jewish immigration, and as boats bringing refugees fleeing from the Nazi threat were turned back or impounded, the Jews intensified their efforts to bring in the immigrants by legal or illegal methods.

In my home town there were also worries, but life went on as normal, despite the arrival in the city of the British Fascist, Oswald Mosley, who held his biggest rally ever, attracting some 10,000 people. If there were two events which should have awoken the world to the dangers to come, it was just weeks before my birth, when Hitler was appointed Führer for life and when over three quarters of a million raised their arms in salute at the Nuremberg Nazi rally.

It was a year of contrasts. The great British composer Sir Edward Elgar died, the King of Yugoslavia was assassinated, and the infamous pair Bonnie and Clyde were shot in Louisiana. Near the town of Wrexham in Wales, 200 men died in a tragic mining disaster. On a happier note, the great liner *Queen Mary* was launched, and Fred Perry won the Wimbledon men's singles tennis title for Britain. Across the Atlantic, the United States had not yet recovered from the great depression and the people tried to enjoy themselves to the music of George Gershwin, singing *I Get a Kick out of You, Blue Moon* and *I Only Have Eyes for You.*

I was barely five years old when Britain and Germany went to war in 1939. I doubt I understood what it was all about at the time, although it became much clearer when enemy aircraft began flying overhead where we lived in Birmingham . The bombs began to rain down on our city, where the factories had been turned over to making arms and munitions for the war effort. As the air-raid sirens wailed out their warnings, we fled to the air-raid shelter and I recall a sense of excitement, even looking forward to descending to the safety of the shelter, the warm blankets and chocolate treats. It was, after all, an adventure.

But this was not to last. I was attending the Hebrew School and together with my teachers and fellow pupils we were packed off to Leicestershire, some forty miles away. We were being evacuated. Complete with just a small suitcase and in anticipation of a gas attack – the square boxed gas mask carried on my shoulder – I was driven the forty miles, a distance in my mind equivalent to 400. My memories of that time are mixed. We were a bunch of eight- to ten-year-old Jewish children who suddenly found ourselves in a small coal-mining village, of warm and extremely kind people who went to church every weekend, and where the men came home from the pit and washed off the soot in a metal bath in the middle of the back kitchen. At last the Allied invasion of France came about and we returned home.

It was in 1945 that I was introduced to Habonim, a Zionist youth group. The object of the movement was to instill a sense of pride in being members of the Jewish people, and prepare us to be ready to shoulder our responsibilities. We were also taught that there is an equal duty for every Jew to be a loyal citizen of the country in which he lives, as well as to encourage a spirit of friendship towards all races and creeds. It was at Habonim that I met my wife, Cynthia, and I suspect that our marriage has reflected some of the foundations we learned there together. Probably it was also at this time that I became a Zionist, without really knowing it. Palestine was another world, the land of the Bible, where Jews had lived for centuries and were now engaged in converting the desert to fertile land, draining the swamps in the north and planting forests to shelter the roads and anchor the soil.

I became aware that the end of the Second World War was going to herald a new era for the world and particularly the Jewish people. Our newspapers, the BBC and the Pathé and Movietone news bulletins at the cinema were dominated, not just by the surrender of the Nazis, but the horrific pictures of the concentration and death camps. Six million Jews as well as Catholics, Gypsies, homosexuals, Freemasons and others who did not fit the Aryan formula had perished, whilst thousands of skeletal human beings sat and crawled into the arms of the rescuing forces of Britain, America and the Soviet Union.

The world was shocked, but not for long. Whilst many survivors from the camps in Europe wanted to leave to be united with families living in Britain and the United States, large numbers wanted to go to Palestine to end their wanderings – the fate of the Jewish people for centuries. Palestine was under the mandate or control of Britain and I had the urge to be able to discuss this explosive situation with the one man who, if he was still alive, might provide an answer. That man was Theodor Herzl, who'd committed his short life to fulfilling, without success in his own lifetime, his Zionist dream.

It was to be some ten years before I could realize my dream.

CHAPTER FIFTEEN

Jerusalem, Israel, 1956

I was just twenty-one when I made my first visit to Israel. The state had been in existence for a rather shorter time, just eight years. My close friend, Leo Cohen, and I had been selected by the Jewish National Fund to make this visit as young emissaries from Britain; to breathe the air of the reborn Jewish homeland and to see the country – from the shores of the Dead Sea in the south to the swamp filled Hula Valley and Lake Kinneret, also known as the Sea of Galilee, in the north. We walked together down the streets of the divided city of Jerusalem, and the entire story of the Bible came to life.

It was difficult not to be completely entranced by the emotion of the pioneering spirit of this young nation and their determination to become a free people once again. This was the country which gave to the world the original collective settlement, the kibbutz. An example too, of Jews whose upright and proud demeanor, looks and attitude flew in the face of the stooped hook-nosed caricatures of the Eastern European Jew as depicted by Nazi and other ill-informed propaganda. Jews who were not just successful bankers, accountants and lawyers, but equally capable of tilling the soil, producing a flourishing and fertile land, and even if ill equipped, of forming an effective defense force.

The five-star King David Hotel stands on King David Street, opposite the YMCA hostel. This contrast of accommodation always struck me as rather amusing and somehow reflected the contrasts in Jewish life. I walked through the legendary and spacious lobby of this famous hotel, built by the Egyptian Moseri family and opened to the public in 1931. I couldn't help my imagination conjuring up images of the world leaders who had visited Palestine in bygone years. Men, and more recently women too, from the great nations of the world assembled in this hotel to discuss the complicated problems of the Middle East – the crossroads of civilization in what appeared unending, unsuccessful and yet optimistic negotiations to secure peace in the region. I decided to have a drink on the terrace which overlooked the historical Old City, divided between Jewish and Jordanian control. I sat down and looked around at the other guests. There was the usual cosmopolitan mixture of western businessmen, several Catholic priests, a group of American tourists and a smattering of Israelis, clearly distinguishable by their casual appearance of open-neck shirts and sports trousers.

I'd ordered an orange juice and sat daydreaming, in the shadow of the tall palm trees, looking over the terrace wall as the sun began to set on the golden skyline of Jerusalem, this capital city of the Bible. I suppose I'd been sitting for about thirty minutes before I became aware of a man sitting opposite me. His black beard and formal coat and trousers did not seem out of place as he removed his silk top hat and placed it on the seat at his side.

"Shalom, my young friend," he said quietly, "I trust you're well and enjoying your visit to the Holy Land." I'd heard the voice before, his appearance was without question.

"Shalom to you too, Theodor," I replied, recognising Herzl.

"I can only assume that the experience for you is somewhat unreal," he remarked. "So much has happened in these last fifty years, we have much to discuss and I'm anxious to learn about the journeys of our people and how this wonderful dream of mine eventually became a reality."

It was going to be a long night and I summoned a waiter and ordered coffee, Israeli salads and some humous and tehina.

"It is fifty-eight years since I was last in Jerusalem, although I visited Egypt in 1903, and whilst I imagine much has changed I suspect a lot remains very much the same. I cannot help but look out at this unique city and feel the impact of history and the peoples who have lived here and made it their home."

We began to discuss the heart of Jerusalem, the Old City. Its stone walls, constructed by the Turks in the sixteenth century and enclosing an area of about one square kilometer, contained the rich history of three of the world's great faiths, Judaism, Christianity and Islam. For 3,000 years the atmosphere of this small area had been charged with these cultures as they lived together, fought against each other, tolerated and hated each other. Here was the site of the sacrifice of Isaac, the location of the crucifixion and resurrection of Jesus and where the prophet Muhammad is said to have ascended to heaven, each reflected in the symbols of the Western Wall, the Church of the Holy Sepulchre and the Dome of the Rock. Could it be anything other than a dream for me to stand alongside this great visionary, and gaze into the capital of the world which had been fought over by so many nations through the generations of time – the Persians, Romans, Crusaders, Turks and, naturally, the Arabs and Jews? We could just see David's Citadel and the Jaffa Gate, one of eight gates which were built as entrances to the Old City.

We stood for some time as we both absorbed this exciting sight. Theodor spoke, "I cannot begin to express my amazement at the sight before my eyes. Continue, please, and tell me, what were the main influences which brought about the foundation of the State of Israel?"

I looked at him and wondered where to start. Herzl had died in 1904 at the age of just forty-four. Since then, history had moved through five decades, two World Wars with horrific results, global economic depressions, the collapse of the mighty British Empire – huge changes in the map of the world and more specific to the question, the rebirth of the Jewish nation. Fortunately for me, the refreshments arrived, the coffee was poured and we began to taste the accompanying food. I gathered my thoughts in an effort to relate to Theodor the significant events which had occurred and had brought us both to this unique place in the center of Jerusalem.

"After 1904, the program of Zionist Congresses continued in cities right across Europe. From Basel, Geneva, and Zürich in Switzerland, to The Hague in Holland; Hamburg and Karlsbad in Germany, in Prague and, you'll be pleased to hear, also in Vienna." He smiled and a quizzical look suggested a missing venue. "Yes, and in 1951 the 23rd Congress finally came home to Jerusalem, as it is again this year in 1956. It was in 1905 that the Jewish National Fund started buying land in Palestine for Jewish settlement, and there were dramatic happenings at the Seventh Congress in that year."

"Which were?"

"You'll recall the British statesman Chamberlain's offer of Jewish settlement in Uganda…" In response to Theodor's nod, I continued, "well, the idea was rejected by the Congress and Israel Zangwill walked out."

"That was sad, because I'm well aware of how difficult it is to repair such damage when strong- minded people make up their minds to take a different road. Chamberlain was a unique influence for us. He understood me completely and what we were seeking and I was convinced that if it were possible, England would find such a place. I'll share a private thought with you, Bernard. He'd nothing against the Jews and if by chance he had one drop of Jewish blood in his veins, he'd have been proud of it, but sadly he hadn't a drop." My look of surprise was accompanied by a comment, "I'm surprised, if not delighted to hear that, because there were other stories which attributed to Chamberlain comments which were distinctly anti-Jewish."

"I can only speak as I found. He always listened with interest to my proposals, showed me great courtesy and I recall that on one occasion this man, whom I would describe as a master figure of England – I suspect you will know how dominant he had become in British politics – showed me to the door and helped me on with my coat. But I've another question perhaps of closer interest: Who became president of the Zionist organization and what other differences emerged?"

"David Wolffsohn succeeded you, and two years later at The Hague Congress there was fresh conflict, this time over the use of Hebrew as the first and official language. I know that you had strong views about this yourself."

"Indeed I did, and I could never quite comprehend this urge to discard the languages of the countries in which Jews had been born and lived for centuries to adopt the language of the Bible. I saw Palestine as a land of Jews and not a Hebrew state."

I thought it better to move our conversation along. "It was in 1911 that the two wings of Zionists found peace, the practical and political groups came together, and even agreed on a session at the Congress being conducted for the first time in Hebrew."

Theodor slowly shook his head before continuing, "I hear all of this, but what of the issue of Palestine? Was it on the agenda of the world powers at the time and what, if any, progress was being made?"

"Yes, it was firmly on the agenda and I'll tell you about it. There continued to be support from the British Government. Dr. Chaim Weizmann, who became the leader of the Zionist movement in 1920 and the first president of Israel in 1948, was becoming a major force in developing Jewish/British relations. He met Arthur James Balfour, the British prime minister, in Manchester, the town where he was living at the time."

Theodor leaned forward to interrupt with a simple question. "This Weizmann, I presume he was the same Weizmann who attended one of the early Congresses, though I can't recall which one. I seem to remember he helped form one of the factions which opposed the way we were proceeding, and I recall that he led a campaign to organize a Conference of Youth."

I paused momentarily, to consider how best to tell Herzl about Weizmann, what a wonderful diplomat he was, and how much he'd achieved in the pursuit of Herzl's Zionist dream, and indeed his own. How could I possibly tell him that there were many who felt Weizmann was in so many ways the architect of the founding of the State of Israel? What Theodor Herzl had started, Chaim Weizmann succeeded in finishing. They were very different men, from different backgrounds with different Jewish foundations, but possibly the most outstanding ambassadors of the Jewish people of their times. Herzl, born in Budapest, brought up in Vienna and well traveled throughout Europe, was an assimilated Jew with little religious knowledge and who mixed with kings and presidents to the exclusion of the masses.

Weizmann was born in Motol, near Pinsk, a *shtetl*, small village in the Russian Pale of Settlement, the very heart of traditional and Orthodox Judaism. He moved to Manchester in 1904, the year Herzl died, and was able to communicate with prime ministers and government leaders as well as with the Jewish masses. Whilst Weizmann was born with Judaism flowing through every vein in his body, it struck Herzl later in life and grew within him. Yet both admired the foundation and culture of Britain. They saw the country as a haven of tolerance and goodwill, and felt that above all others, the British government was the one most likely to support their vision of a Jewish national home in Palestine.

Herzl saw his dream as one of territory, a haven from anti-Semitism for the Jewish people. Weizmann viewed the Jewish national home as a historical and religious link between the Jewish people and the ancient Land of Israel. And yet they were so alike. They shared a love of the Jewish people and both earned their respect. They dedicated their lives to the achievement of an almost impossible dream and whilst Herzl, like Moses, did not live to see it achieved, Weizmann was blessed to walk and live in the Promised Land.

"Weizmann did not attend the first Congress in Basel and I suspect that this was because he couldn't afford to do so, and in any case he was deeply involved with his research in chemistry. He did attend the second Congress in 1898. It was three years later that he did help to establish the Democratic Fraction, which he and his friends intended to be totally loyal to the Zionist dream, yet opposed to your way of working. Their objective was to respond to the mood of the masses, recognizing the cultural and colonization aspirations. He was a great Zionist, he thought the world of you and it was because he had a different background that he found himself somewhat opposed to your style. Let's say that he felt a little out of touch with the way you handled matters, but without a doubt, he shared your ambition to establish a Jewish home in Palestine."

"So what was so different?" demanded Theodor. "It was this attitude of some of our people which made our work so difficult. Why couldn't he join us in a united drive, rather than split the ranks which always makes achieving support so much more difficult?"

This was a deeply searching question from someone who clearly had died disappointed, with his ambitions unrealized. I felt unable to adequately answer.

"Thanks to your efforts, progress did in fact begin to be made. Weizmann became a highly respected biochemist and made a valuable contribution to British science. He was able to build on his reputation and relationships with a whole range of leading national figures and politicians. This came to the fore when the First World War broke out in 1914, when his contribution to the war effort was greatly appreciated."

A strange look came over Theodor's face reminding me that he would be totally unaware of this, or indeed of future wars, which had engulfed most of the world.

"This war was known as the Great War. It began in 1914 and lasted for four years. It had been prompted by the assassination of the Archduke Francis Ferdinand, heir to the Hapsburg throne, and then through Germany's declaration of war against Russia and France and the subsequent invasion of Belgium. Great Britain then declared war on Germany, resulting in a bloody conflict which claimed sixteen million lives." With this brief explanation

I continued, "It was in this period that Weizmann's influence began to bear fruit. He was able to develop his relationship with Mr. Balfour, the foreign minister, and created such an impression on Mr. C.P. Scott, the editor of the *Manchester Guardian* [now the *Guardian*] that both he and his close friend Mr. David Lloyd George, the prime minister, became Zionists."

"So where did all this friendship lead to?"

"In 1917, Weizmann, who had been elected the president of the British Zionist organization, almost single-handedly succeeded in getting the British government to make a historic statement, called the Balfour Declaration, about Britain's commitment to the establishment of a Jewish National Home in Palestine."

Theodor sat back in his seat, tears appearing in his eyes, as he realized the significance of this event. He said quietly, "What did this statement or declaration, as you call it, say?"

"It came in the form of a letter from Arthur James Balfour, the British foreign minister, to Lord Rothschild." At the sound of the name, Theodor raised his eyebrows with interest as he leaned forward in his chair. "He wrote that he wished to convey on behalf of His Majesty's Government a declaration of sympathy with the Jewish Zionist aspirations, one which had the support of the cabinet. This declaration viewed with favor the establishment in Palestine of a national home for the Jewish people and the government undertook to use its best endeavors to facilitate the achievement of this objective."

Theodor stood up and went over to the window to gaze out onto the Old City of Jerusalem as he seemed lost in thought. He turned and walked back towards me. He seemed to have grown in stature as he looked down with a look of pride on his face. "Amazing, amazing," he repeated, "what an achievement. Weizmann and his friends had been right to reject Uganda, but go on. Was this an unconditional commitment, or were there conditions?"

"Indeed there were; Balfour's letter required that nothing should be done which might prejudice the civil and religious rights of existing non-Jewish communities in Palestine, or the rights and political status enjoyed by Jews in any other country."

Theodor nodded as I continued. "This Declaration was not achieved without considerable struggles within the Anglo-Jewish community. Whilst the Jews living in London's East End, many of them refugees from Russia and Eastern Europe, supported the Zionist objective with passion, the so-called 'establishment' opposed it. They were fewer in numbers, but greater in influence, and Weizmann had to contend with this opposition, generated via letters to the British press and the briefing of cabinet ministers with whom the leadership of British Jews had close contact."

Theodor smiled as he shook his head. "Weizmann had the same problems I faced, and I can well understand his frustration with this enemy from within."

"Theodor, you'll be pleased to learn that one of the great names supporting Weizmann and the Zionist dream was Lord Rothschild. One of the fiercest opponents was Edwin Montagu, a wealthy Jewish member of the cabinet – himself the target of anti-Semitism – who'd fiercely opposed the Balfour commitment at every opportunity in the cabinet, but thankfully his efforts failed. Montagu went off to be the secretary of state for India and it was left to Lloyd George and Balfour to make sure that the British government honored its pledge."

"I never cease to be grateful to those non-Jews in our midst, who have so often been our finest supporters, whereas the assimilated Jews rely on their wealth and complacency to believe they'll always be protected from anti-Semitism."

It seemed appropriate to say nothing further, as we both sat quietly considering the impact of this letter of just 120 or so words which had such a dramatic impact on history, and which had started the course of the establishment of Israel and the conflict and pain which followed.

A waiter hovered in the background and I summoned him over, asking Theodor if he'd like a drink or some refreshment. He smiled and nodding his head said, "I think it's timely and perhaps as your story has reached such an exciting stage, I'll take a brandy with some cake." I gave the order to the waiter, adding a coffee and some apple strudel for myself.

"Let's move on. I'm sure that this Balfour Declaration was just the start."

"The World War drew to an end and with Turkey defeated, Britain's General Allenby marched into Judea, captured Jerusalem and subsequently occupied Palestine. The Jews who had been expelled from Tel Aviv and Jaffa by the Turks returned, and hopes were again raised by a Zionist Commission headed by Weizmann."

"Palestine has certainly had more than its fair share of commissions and I just wonder about the result of this one," smiled Theodor.

"The whole issue of Palestine was referred to the League of Nations which decided to award the mandate of Palestine to Britain in 1920. This was the start of a period of considerable differences, even acrimony, between Jews and the British government, and was destined to last for twenty-six years. That is in itself a long story, so perhaps we should take some rest and continue tomorrow."

"You're right, we've talked enough for today, and despite your being so young, I feel we're both tired. Let's retire and meet tomorrow when you can continue this wonderful story, and perhaps you'll also tell me about how the Zissmans came to England, for I suspect your grandparents may well have come from another land."

CHAPTER SIXTEEN

Biala Podlaska, 1853

The following morning dawned bright and sunny as I strolled from a meeting at Keren Hayesod in the Jewish Agency building, through the Jerusalem streets which reflected the history of the Jewish people and the country's extraordinary relationship with Great Britain. Jabotinsky Street, named for an inspirational Zionist leader, and King George, Balfour and Disraeli streets, named in honor of the British monarch and two great statesmen.

I found Theodor sitting quietly in the lounge of the King David Hotel. We greeted each other with the traditional Israeli "shalom", before he spoke. "I've spent the last hours since we met reflecting on what you've told me and I'm excited, as well as apprehensive, to hear you continue. But before that, I want to hear about you, your family's journey, where you came from, and how you came to be here in Jerusalem at this time."

＊　＊　＊

This is a story of sadness and of courage, of hope and dreams, and whilst it is my story, it is also the story of thousands of others who were born in Eastern Europe and felt that their future lay in a freer country across the seas. So as Theodor Herzl sat quietly in a chair listening, I began my tale.

"It is 1853, in a town called Biala Podlaska in Russian Poland, over 1,000 miles from where we sit today, 100 miles east of Warsaw and seventy-five miles north of Lublin. You recall what was happening in the Jewish communities of Eastern European, the pogroms, the oppression and the incessant anti-Semitism."

Theodor nodded, but didn't interrupt.

"The town was not large and, like most Polish towns, was dominated by a central square. On one side of the square were the municipal offices whilst the other sides were occupied by the town's library, an elegant building known as Radziwill's Palace and a number of official-looking buildings including a rather attractive 17th-century church. They varied in height and were gray in color and appearance, and somehow reflected the atmosphere and appearance of the local citizens who seemed to go about their business with heavy feet as well as heavy hearts. It was a depressing scene.

"Biala Podlaska was a military garrison town and the sound of army boots would more often than not be heard pounding the streets.

"A baby boy was born named Joseph Abraham Zissman and that baby was my great-grandfather. Life for the Jews was not good in those days in that part of Eastern Europe. The Crimean War was under way. My family was involved with the revolutionary movement of the time and the men fought in several unsuccessful attempts to overthrow Russian rule.

"The family head, Jacob Zissman, worked as a cap-maker, most of what he made going to the army. He owned a horse and cart and used it to transport his merchandise to Brest Litovsk, just across the Russian border. These visits enabled him to buy essential household items such as paraffin and other produce, which he was able to sell to the Jewish community at home.

"There was great excitement in the Zissman home. The family was a very traditional Eastern European Jewish family. The men, Chassidim, were dressed in long black coats and large-brimmed fur hats, rather like some men you can still see in parts of the East End of London or New York. The arrival of a baby son was confirmation that the family line would continue, and on the eighth day after Joseph's birth it was time for the traditional ceremony of the *brit mila*, the circumcision. The family had gathered from throughout the region for what was to be a happy occasion, not just for the Zissman family, but for the whole community.

"There had been rumors for some time that Jewish communities in the region were being threatened, attacked and even imprisoned. Like most rumors, they were dismissed by our family, as they seemed protected from such troubles, but the peace was soon to be broken.

"Suddenly there was the sound of shouting and screaming in the street, the thud of horses' hooves on the cobbles outside, and a terrified silence came over the whole house. The door was banged once, then again and again, and as nobody rushed to open it, the door finally burst open. Standing there were five or six, possibly more, of the czar's soldiers, dressed in Cossack fur hats, brown coats buttoned to the neck and high black leather boots.

"They were rampaging through the village seeking out Jewish homes to burn and pillage. They pushed into our small home, brushing aside those who stood in their way and seized Jacob, my great-great-grandfather. Despite the cries and protestations of the family and particularly of his wife, who was still in bed not yet fully recovered from the birth, they took him away, away from the warmth of his family, right in front of his newborn son who was about to be initiated into the Jewish faith. Women fainted; men rushed to try and protect him, but to no avail. He was dragged into the street and, together with men from other homes, thrown into the back of a carriage.

"He was never again seen as were many of the menfolk of Biala Podlaska. The next 20 years were hard for the Zissman family. They were a learned family and my great-grandfather received a basic education in secular subjects and a fairly advanced religious education.

"During the mid-19th century many Jewish families attempted to flee from Eastern Europe to the more accommodating parts of

Europe, and those with adventure in their blood sought out the Americas. In 1873 my great-grandfather married Sophie. It was one of the happier moments in the family history but the following day was one of pain as well as joy. The young Joseph and Sophie had planned to leave the stark and oppressive environment of Biala, and the day after their wedding they secretly left the village in which they had both grown up to seek a new life in the United States. They had saved a modest amount of money and managed to secure from a local broker two tickets on a boat which left from Gdansk the following week. Their journey to the port was a frightening experience as they sheltered during the day, traveling only at night to avoid the bandits and soldiers who were rife at that time and on the lookout for young Poles fleeing the country. They reached Gdansk and managed to embark on the boat which they understood was destined for New York and for which they had bought tickets. But they had been cheated and the boat went only as far as Tilbury, just down the River Thames. From there they traveled to London. They sat huddled together in the train, hardly able to say anything. The other passengers stared at them with incredulity; their clothing looked strange and they obviously spoke very little English. They did however successfully complete the journey, becoming two of the two million or so Jews who fled from Eastern Europe to England and the United States, ending up finding a home with Joseph's brother, Hershel, in Brick Lane in the East End of London.

"My grandfather, Myer, was born in 1884 in Brick Lane, at that time the center of the Jewish settlement in London. He was an ambitious man and not really content to being confined to work in the cramped family premises. So my grandfather decided in 1906 that he would seek his fortune in the industrial north of the country and, boarding a train, he alighted at Birmingham, a thriving Midlands city where he observed a large male population all wearing hats and caps. This, he decided, was the place for Myer Zissman, a cap maker by trade, so he settled in Birmingham, bringing his wife, Julie, who subsequently bore him a son – my father – and two daughters.

"I must tell you of another strange coincidence. My grandfather, just 22 years old, arrived at Birmingham's elegant Snow Hill Station from Paddington in London and made his way up one the city's main streets, Colmore Row. He passed through Victoria Square in which stood the resplendent statue of the Queen for whom it was named and looked up at the imposing Council House, home of Birmingham's municipal government. He was impressed by this building, designed by Yeoville Thomason, who had also designed the Singers Hill Synagogue, barely a mile away in the original Jewish quarter of the city. He had no reason to think he would ever climb the steps, or that any of his descendants would. It would have surprised him, and hopefully given him pride, to know that his grandson was to become the 78th Lord Mayor of Birmingham eighty-four years later.

"Myer Zissman walked on, glancing at the Town Hall, a concert hall built in the style of the great Coliseum of Rome, as he followed hundreds of local citizens journeying to a political meeting being held in Bingley Hall. This is the former home of the Lloyd banking family, later used as a meeting place and exhibition hall, and on that day the scene of an important announcement. As my grandfather, along with the rest of the audience, stood waiting patiently, they were suddenly swept up in a roar of a cheering as an elderly handsome man, smartly dressed with a monocle in his right eye and an orchid in his black jacket lapel, strode on to the stage. The gathering fell silent as he spoke, announcing his retirement from politics. That man was Joseph Chamberlain, the man you met; the man who impressed you and whom you considered a friend of the Jewish people."

*   *   *

Theodor looked at me with a knowing look on his face. "Amazing, isn't it, that both your grandfather and I should have been in the company of this great British statesman. I would have recognized him from the description of the orchid and monocle. Your family has indeed traveled the traditional Jewish journey. I recall vividly my visit to Vilna, also in Russian Poland, where, as you know, I was greeted by the Jewish population with so much joy and enthusiasm, something I really didn't feel comfortable with, and where I learned first-hand of the suffering of our people and about life in the ghetto. We've been fleeing for generations and it's time we settled down. From the time of the Bible when we were attacked by the Assyrians and Babylonians, when Judas Maccabaeus fought valiantly against the conquering Greeks, followed by the mighty Roman Empire's destruction of the Second Temple, we've been wandering. Even our great contribution to Spain's culture did not save us from being expelled in 1492, and we fared little better in France, and your own country, who banished the Jews in the 13th century. But enough of that, let's continue to look forward. So, what brings you to Israel?"

CHAPTER SEVENTEEN

Jerusalem, Israel, 1956

I explained to Theodor how I came to be in Jerusalem with my friend, Leo Cohen, and the excitement and feeling of "belonging" we were both experiencing since our arrival in the Holy Land.

"We left our conversation at the point when the issue of Palestine was before the League of Nations. Great Britain had been entrusted in 1920, via a mandate, with the control of land far beyond what we now know as the borders. It stretched from the Mediterranean Sea in the west to Syria in the north, Iraq in the northeast, Saudi Arabia to the east and south, and Egypt in the southwest."

Theodor asked, "And was this mandate, as you call it, endorsed by the nations of the world?"

"Yes it was, and there was a significant result as far as you are concerned. A year earlier, in 1919, the Paris Peace Conference of all the nations involved in the conflict met to settle issues arising from the end of the World War and accepted the promise made by the Balfour Declaration to the establishment of a Jewish National Home in Palestine."

"Twenty-two long and traumatic years after our first Zionist Congress in Basel, the dream was beginning to come true," exclaimed Theodor, with an uncharacteristic look of satisfaction on his face.

"Yes, but some felt that Britain was promising the same land to different people. A few years later the government established, quite

151

unilaterally, the Emirate of Transjordan on the eastern side of the River Jordan and the Dead Sea, and planted the seeds of the conflict which was to follow. Whilst the foreign secretary had clearly promised Palestine, or part of it, to the Jews, in the Balfour Declaration, the British high commissioner in Egypt was making a pledge to the Arabs to establish an Arab Kingdom in the very same piece of land."

Theodor raised his hand. "Did this promise describe the borders of such a kingdom?"

"Sadly it didn't, referring only to Arab western Asia, and rather like Balfour's equally vague statement about a Jewish home, left the definition of boundaries undecided."

"A recipe, it seems to me, for disaster and conflict," he suggested, with a hint of prophesy in his words.

"It certainly was. Within a couple of years there were Arab riots in Jaffa and this led to a period of fighting between Arab and Jew and even to the expulsion of Jews from parts of the country. But there was more encouraging news in this period too. In 1920, the British government sent a former cabinet minister who was Jewish, Sir Herbert Samuel, to be the first high commissioner of Palestine. Meanwhile, Weizmann, forever in search of peaceful solutions, and a few months before being elected to the presidency of the Zionist Organization, went to meet King Feisal of Iraq."

Theodor nodded. "That sounds very interesting. I hesitate to ask about the results of these developments."

"Neither brought much success. Some years later, after his return to England, Samuel, who by then was a member of the House of Lords, argued for the creation of a confederation of Arab states within which would exist a Jewish national home. This was all the more surprising, as it was in the parliamentary debate which proposed the partition of Palestine between Arab and Jewish states – following the recommendation of yet another commission, this one led by Lord Peel."

"And what about the Feisal meeting? I have to admit that my own meetings with Eastern heads of state proved to be both frustrating and unrewarding."

"Good question, and if only this meeting could have delivered its ambition. Weizmann and King Feisal did actually sign an agreement in January 1919 about the Zionist colonization of Palestine. One of its clauses set a timetable to agree the boundaries between the Arab and Jewish states, and another committed to increased and speedy Jewish immigration, in order to cultivate the land. The King followed this meeting with a meaningful letter which he wrote to a Mr. Felix Frankfurter." I could see the question on Theodor's face as I sought to explain. "Frankfurter was an American appointed member of the Paris Peace Conference and met King Feisal as a result of an introduction by the immortal Lawrence of Arabia. The King wrote that educated Arabs were in sympathy with the Zionist ideals, and felt that the two peoples could work together to establish a working relationship in the region."

As my mind raced forward in time and dwelt on these ambitions of such huge goodwill between Arab and Jew and how time had turned them on their head, Theodor murmured, "If only those wise words would come true."

"Wise words *were* being said by all concerned. The Twelfth Zionist Congress approved a resolution which called on Jews to live in harmony and mutual respect with the Arab people, and one only has to look around now, in 1956, to see how history has judged those words."

"Perhaps earlier generations of both peoples were wiser than yours – but tell me about Jewish immigration to Palestine, for the life blood of any nation is people, especially young people, and without that essential ingredient, no country can grow."

I spent the next half an hour detailing the waves of *aliya*, immigration from different parts of Europe, much of it encouraged and funded by Baron Rothschild. Following the first aliya in 1882, some were, fleeing persecution and prompted by the socialist Zionist ideas of Moses Hess about redeeming the soil, the second wave of some 40,000 came in 1905, and followed the failed Russian revolution. It was in this period, the early 1900s, that David Ben-Gurion, Joseph Trumpeldor, Yitzhak Ben-Zvi, Vladimir Jabotinsky and Levi Eshkol came to Palestine and created the foundation of the new leadership. The year 1919, after the end of the First World War, brought the beginning of the new immigration and this was followed in 1925 from Poland and another wave in 1933 as Jews began to flee from the Nazi oppression in Central Europe. The result of this was that in the three years between 1933 and 1935, nearly 150,000 immigrants came to Palestine, doubling the Jewish population of the country. Twenty years later, in 1956, the population of Israel numbered some 1.8 million.

Theodor listened closely, and then asked, with doubt in his voice, "Was all of this immigration welcomed by the Arabs and the nations of the West?"

"No. This was part of the cause of the riots we spoke of before, and there were continued clashes between Jews and Arabs. In 1922, the British government issued a White Paper, a document setting out proposed government policy. Whilst this recognized that the Jews were in Palestine 'of right and not under sufferance', it nevertheless restricted Jewish immigration, which would only be permitted as long as it didn't exceed the economic capacity of the country. What was surprising was that this was presented to parliament by colonial secretary Winston Churchill, who was one of the strongest supporters of the Zionist ambition. This was a man who, years later in the British House of Commons, referred to the State of Israel as 'an event in world history to be viewed in the perspective not of a generation, or of a century, but in the perspective of a thousand years, two thousand years or even three thousand years'. This White Paper which he presented also sought to clarify some of the confusion in the Balfour Declaration."

"And was that helpful?"

"Not really, because it only added further confusion by speaking of Jews taking pride in the development of a Jewish center in Palestine."

"So no clearer definition of borders?" questioned Theodor. "What did our people think of all of this?"

"They accepted this situation somewhat unhappily, but reacted much more strongly to Sir Herbert Samuel's decision to halt all immigration in 1921 in the face of repeated Arab unrest. As the number of immigrants continued to rise during the twenties and early thirties, the Arabs became even more hostile to the Jews, as well as rebelling against the British and calling general strikes."

As Theodor listened quietly I told him of the political changes also taking place in the Arab world. In 1925, France gave Lebanon greater autonomy and brought together the districts of Damascus and Aleppo to create Syria. Eight years later, Britain granted independence to Iraq, appointed Feisal as king, who then named his brother, Abdullah, as Emir of Transjordan.

"These changes must have had some impact? "

"They did, and primarily they raised the hopes of both the Arabs and Jews that promises already given by the Balfour Declaration, as well as other pledges, would lead to the establishment of Jewish and Arab Palestinian states."

Doubt appeared on Theodor's face and he stroked his beard. "I suspect that didn't happen."

"No, all it did was to create animosity of both Jews and Arabs to Britain, which was anxious to retain the traditional goodwill of the Arabs – to preserve the supplies of oil, whilst recognizing the growing plight of the Jews in Europe. It was in 1939 that the British government made its biggest *volte face* when a further White Paper was published – in response to yet a another commission on Palestine – and which went back on the promise made by Balfour of a Jewish National Home. Despite all of the horror stories coming out of Germany and the neighboring countries, about the rise of the conquering Nazis and imprisonment of hundreds of thousands of Jews, the British government decided to restrict Jewish immigration to Palestine to just 10,000 a year for five years, plus a special allowance of 25,000 refugees."

Theodor shook his head. "I think I can guess, but please confirm why they took such a strange and cruel decision."

"To satisfy the Arabs that the intention was to establish an independent Palestine which would have an Arab majority who would have the final say on the number of Jews entering the country."

"I can imagine the disappointment felt by the Zionist leadership, because I too had suffered such disappointments. My heart bleeds for those left to the dangers to which you've referred. You spoke earlier of this plight and of the immigration from Europe when Jews were fleeing from the Nazis. I'm not sure I fully understand the significance of this period."

I realized that with all we'd talked about, I'd failed to make Theodor aware of one of the most traumatic periods in Jewish as well as world history, and I paused for a few moments to try and find appropriate words. I started to speak in a hushed tone. "You were well aware of the evils of anti-Semitism and experienced its impact in Vienna and in Paris. It was in Vienna that one of the greatest evils of my time erupted with the growth of the Nazis under the leadership of Adolf Hitler, and which spread like a cancer across the whole of Europe from its base in Germany."

As Theodor listened, captivated with a look of horror on his face, I explained the tragedy of the Second World War, how it had engulfed nearly every country from America to Australia, and how Japan and Italy had entered the conflict on the side of the Nazis. He slumped back in his chair as I shared with him graphic details of the concentration and extermination camps, sealing the fate of six million Jews in what history has termed the Holocaust.

"I cannot begin to comprehend the impact on so many generations of our people..." and as he paused, he thought, perhaps, of his dream being realized so much sooner, leaving unsaid the words 'what if', before he asked, "So what of the people in Palestine during this terrible conflict, did they participate in any way?"

"A very different situation developed between the Jews and the Arabs. Members of the underground Hagana's Palmach elite strike force volunteered to form a Jewish fighting force within the British army, but it wasn't until September 1944 that Churchill announced in Parliament the establishment of a Jewish Brigade as part of the Allied army. By contrast, the mufti of Jerusalem was in Berlin pledging the support of the Arabs for the Nazi cause."

We helped ourselves to a fresh cup of coffee as I continued to explain developments in Palestine.

"The end of the war signaled fresh efforts to establish a Jewish home as the British Mandate of Palestine entered its dying and painful days. News reached England daily of attacks on British forces by the Jewish resistance – termed freedom fighters by some and terrorists by others, depending on your point of view. Thousands of Jews, including many members of the Zionist leadership, were arrested and incarcerated, prisons were bombed and innocent men and women died, some just doing their duty, others caught up in this period of 'tit for tat' killing. There was a huge build-up of feeling right across the world as the British government, under the unrelenting and unsympathetic hand of foreign secretary Ernest Bevin, resisted plea after plea to allow greater Jewish immigration to Palestine. Thousands of displaced refugees from Europe sailing in all sizes of ships seeking a new home and a new life were imprisoned on the island of Cyprus, under the guard of the same British soldiers who had a year or so earlier released them from the Bergen-Belsen concentration camp. Others were returned to their original countries, the notable example being the ship *Exodus,* which was sent back with 4,500 refugees from Poland and Germany. Another ship, which you may be interested to learn, was named *Theodor Herzl,* and arrived at Haifa in July 1947, bearing a banner, 'The Germans destroyed our families and homes, don't destroy our hopes."

Theodor looked at me with what appeared a tear in his eye, "Tragic, tragic indeed. When these boats started their journey they must have appeared like luxury liners taking their passengers to a new land, and a new life. What a tragedy that they became ships destined to return to hell. It's hard to contemplate the feeling of despair and agony, not to say anger, which must have prevailed on board."

"There were passionate speeches in the British House of Commons, one of the most memorable from Richard Crossman, a non-Jew and leading member of the Labor Party, which was the government of the day."

Theodor raised his head to ask, "And what was so special about this speech?"

"He was speaking to a mainly hostile Parliament, saying it was impossible to crush a resistance movement which had the support of the mass of people. Arresting thousands of people would serve no useful purpose; neither would the continued and unjustified ban on Jewish immigration. Dr. Weizmann, who had escaped capture because he was abroad at the time, expressed his deep concern. He spoke of acts of Jewish 'terrorism' which he said sprang from despair of ever securing a home or justice via peaceful means."

"Are these not the words which will be recognized by anyone who has studied the birth of a new nation, and no doubt will be used by those Arabs who feel themselves displaced?"

I didn't see the need to challenge what was turning out to be an accurate observation, as I continued to recount what happened next. "The climax of the conflict came on July 22, 1946, with the bombing by the Jewish armed group Irgun Zva'i Leumi, of the hotel in which we now sit. An entire wing of the King David had been commandeered by the British as their military and administrative headquarters, and the Jews felt that a strike at the very heart of British authority would send a message directly to London. Over ninety people were killed including British administrators, Arabs and Jews – even a refugee who had survived the Nazis only to be killed by fellow Jews."

"I suspect that the reaction of the British, like most colonial powers, was fairly swift and harsh."

"The shock waves raced around the world and the act was condemned by Jew and non-Jew alike. David Ben-Gurion, who had spent his life driving forward the Zionist cause and was destined to become Israel's first prime minister, was in Paris at the time, and joined in the condemnation, going as far as to describe the Irgun as the enemy of the Jewish people. In Palestine there was disarray between the various Jewish resistance groups and the military coalition collapsed. The more moderate Hagana, formed in the 1920s to protect Jewish settlements against Arab attacks, concentrated on bringing illegal immigrants to Palestine whilst Lehi, known in the western world as the Stern Gang, and the Irgun continued their controversial military struggle. There were two other significant events which influenced the speed of disorder rapidly engulfing the country. The British intensified their oppressive activity with widescale arrests and curfews and, following the King David outrage, General Sir Evelyn Barker made a huge blunder by issuing a statement with anti-Semitic overtones."

"I find that hard to believe from a British soldier whose discipline with both the gun and the word is renowned. What on earth did he say?"

"He issued orders that all military personnel were to boycott Jewish shops and hit what he called 'this race where it hurts most, in their pocket.'"

Theodor shook his head. "What a surprising thing to say. I can well imagine how much damage this caused. But what was the other significant event about which you spoke?"

I went on to describe the horror of the murder by the Irgun of two British sergeants in retaliation for the killing of Jewish terrorists, and lurid pictures of the soldiers found hanging in an orange grove printed on the front page of every British newspaper. In many ways these events were to be the nadir of British rule. Calls to bring home the troops were loud and clear and it seemed to me that the British public, in looking at both the Arabs and Jews, were saying 'a plague on both your houses.'

"It was in 1947 that the nations of the world, now under the banner of the United Nations, began to debate what was to change forever the map of the Middle East and set in place a new conflict which exists to this day and may well continue for some decades to come."

We'd been sitting for some time in the King David lounge and I suggested that perhaps we take a walk and continue our conversation in the fresh air. We passed through the foyer and this time I watched as Theodor looked with interest at the guests dressed rather more informally than he was accustomed to seeing.

We turned left outside the hotel and strolled up King David Street towards its junction with Keren Hayesod Street. We stopped for a moment to gaze over what was known as "no man's land", as I pointed out a tract of uncultivated sand and rubble land only yards wide which separated Israel from Jordan.

"Let me tell you about what happened on November 29, 1947. Every Jewish home sat listening to the radio as the 128th session of the United Nations General Assembly, held at Flushing Meadow, New York, was in progress. The proposal under debate was the partition of Palestine into two states, one Jewish, the other Arab. One of the surprises came from the delegate of the Soviet Union, Andrei Gromyko, later to become foreign minister, who spoke strongly in support of the Jewish state. This meant that the two major world nations, the United States of America and the Soviet Union, so often opposed on a range of issues, were united in support of the partition resolution. The United States, however, was suggesting that part of the Negev in the south be given to the Arabs, but France expressed doubts. Weizmann and Ben-Gurion, even though they had fallen out in terms of approach, worked tirelessly to persuade the United States, France and other doubting nations of the justice of the Jewish case."

The raised eyebrows again expressed Theodor's view. "Our leadership never fails to amaze me with its internal struggles. However, these matters are never straightforward, and I'm doubtful whether one can always trust the word of even the most upright of politicians. But please continue."

"While the vote was under way, Weizmann sat quietly in his room at the New York Plaza Hotel, overlooking Central Park. It was a cliffhanger. To succeed, the proposal needed a two-thirds majority and it was known that a number of countries, including

the United Kingdom, would abstain. Those who sat by their ra-
dios listened intently as the votes were announced in alphabeti-
cal order. It was a bad start; Afghanistan voted 'no' and Argentina
abstained. Matters improved as Australia, Belgium, Bolivia and
Brazil all voted 'yes'. There was high drama as one by one the nations of the world announced their vote. Not unexpectedly, the
Arab-affiliated and sympathetic delegates all voted against, until
we reached the United Kingdom, which abstained. The United
States voted 'yes'. Finally, the Brazilian president of the General
Assembly, Mr. Aranha, announced that the proposal to partition
Palestine between Jewish and Arab states had been approved by
33 votes in favor with 13 against and 10 abstentions. Dr. Weizmann
received the news with deep emotion and joy. He then left for
Carnegie Hall to greet a large Zionist audience who welcomed
him with rapturous applause. His dark glasses just managed to
conceal his tears."

We stood together looking at the divided city as we both
thought deeply about a new era in Jewish and world history. "What
an achievement," came Theodor's simple comment. "I'm full of
admiration for the efforts of the Zionist leadership, Weizmann
and Ben-Gurion, and presumably so many others who put their
political and personal weight behind the proposal."

"It was touch and go for many days, weeks and months prior
to the United Nations vote. The British government had had
enough. It seemed to many observers at the time that they wanted
to get out of Palestine with all possible speed and leave the problem with the United Nations. It always seemed to me a tragedy that
the country which had done so much to bring about the establishment of a Jewish national home had ended its control in such
disarray. Across the ocean, the United States was also being tested.
President Truman, who had supported partition, was unimpressed
with the continual criticism of his administration by American
Zionists and subsequently wavered. It was only the intervention of
American Zionist leaders Dewey Stone and Frank Goldman who,
via a friend of the president, Eddie Jacobson, secured a meeting in

the Oval Office for Weizmann which secured the continued but vital support of the United States."

The October evening was beginning to become chilly, and I felt it time to end this conversation. This view was not shared by Theodor, who began to press me for more information about what happened after the dramatic partition vote. "Perhaps we'll retire to the hotel lounge and I'll continue the story. There's so much to tell."

We walked back, retracing our steps, as I explained about the one point where you could cross between Jordan and Israel, the Mandelbaum Gate, which was guarded by Arab and Israeli marksmen.

"I can only assume that the period following the decision of the world's nations was neither easy nor peaceful," Herzl remarked. I felt that this perceptive observation demanded some answers. "It was on Friday May 14, 1948, at around four o'clock in the after-noon, just before the start of the Sabbath, in a small building in Tel Aviv – I think in use as a museum – that David Ben-Gurion in front of a small gathering, which included future president Yitzhak Ben-Zvi and future prime ministers Moshe Shertok [later Sharett] and Golda Meir, announced the independence of the State of Israel, described as the first independent Jewish state for nearly two thousand years. Later that day, and as the British mandate was coming to an end, the United States of America recognized the young nation, following the Soviet Union, which was the first government to do so. President Truman signed a simple docu-ment in which he had struck out the words 'new Jewish State' and inserted 'new State of Israel.'"

"I suppose we'd now have a new nation of Israelites," remarked Theodor, at which I smiled before answering. "Not so. The foreign minister, Moshe Shertok, announced the following Thursday that Israelites were the people of the Bible; that Israel was a modern nation and its citizens would be Israelis."

I went on to explain that two of the first proclamations were that Israel would be open to every Jew who wished to immigrate, and that friendship was offered to the neighboring Arab nations. My listener expressed his shock when told about the immediate invasion – on the very day after independence was proclaimed – by Egypt, Iraq, Jordan, Lebanon and Syria. What I had not yet explained was the totally unfair borders produced by the partition plan, which left the Jewish State with an area equivalent only to the size of the State of New Jersey in the USA or Wales in the UK, and in some places just thirteen kilometers wide.

"This war, about which you speak, presumably the War of Independence, would no doubt have come to an end and hopefully would result in some form of peaceful existence between Israel and her neighbors – even though I can see from our conversation and looking across the border that, after eight years, the solution hasn't yet been found."

How could I, with the benefit of foresight, give the comfort being sought when I knew that Israel was destined to live through not just eight but more than fifty-eight years of conflict, continual battles and war? I reflected on the Sinai Campaign which would start within days of our meeting, to the 1967 Six Day War, which astounded the world, particularly military strategists, who watched how Israel in a pre-emptive strike against its surrounding enemies completely destroyed the Arab air forces before a single plane left the ground. And then to the Yom Kippur War of 1973, and onwards, and onwards, to more bitter unconventional conflicts, not previously known to mankind and destined to bring pain and distress for Israel as well as her neighboring citizens.

Seeing the doubts on my face, Theodor ended our conversation with a few thoughtful words. "Nothing which is valuable is gained easily or without considerable sacrifice or pain. I've always believed that Palestine is our unforgettable historical homeland. To live as free men on our own soil and die in our own homes may well take time, more than either you or I may have, but in the end, peace will prevail and whatever benefit we achieve for ourselves will rebound with huge benefit for all mankind."

CHAPTER EIGHTEEN

London, England, 2006

March 2006 in London turned out to be colder than normal, with the signs of overdue rain signaling the end of a drought, more common in Israel's Negev desert than the green fields of England.

I walked through one of the two sets of revolving doors of the Savoy Hotel, located for the last 117 years in London's Strand, and strolled through the elegant foyer down the nine steps to the Thames Foyer where afternoon tea was served. I was shown to a table as the pianist, seated in the centre of the room, played *A Nightingale Sang in Berkeley Square*. I sat and waited for my guest, who I knew had last been in the Savoy Hotel in 1896 and would find our meeting place interesting, as well as a reminder of his memorable address to a packed meeting in the East End of London.

I looked around the elegant lounge, whose walls no doubt could tell some astounding stories from the visits of Sarah Bernhardt, Lillie Langtry and the Prince of Wales, through the era of Sir Winston Churchill and Mrs Eleanor Roosevelt to Elizabeth Taylor, Charlie Chaplin and Marilyn Monroe. My guest wouldn't have seen the colourful Art Deco mirrors installed around 1930, or the more recent murals of the countryside, all of which added to the sheer elegance and luxury of this setting.

I watched carefully for the arrival of my guest. Theodor Herzl would not be late, and as I observed him walking towards me down the stairs, passing the imposing floral display of white roses, lilies and yellow forsythia. I wasn't surprised to note that whilst he had removed his silk top hat, his formal clothes were in no way out of place among the traditional morning dress and black evening suits of the hotel staff. I rose; we greeted each other warmly, and I invited him to take a seat.

The waiter served the traditional English tea which had been a specialty of the Savoy Hotel since its inception, although we could have chosen from a huge range of teas and infusions. A simple cup of tea seems to have become such a complicated matter. The waiter deposited on the table a three-tiered stand of delicious-looking pastries, which accompanied a range of small sandwiches, scones and even tea cakes.

Tea having been served, and after some time spent glancing around at our fellow guests, Theodor spoke. "Bernard, we last met together in Jerusalem fifty years ago. You were making your first visit to Israel and had explained how the state came to be founded. Much will have happened since then and I'm anxious to hear how our young nation progressed, hopefully becoming an example to others, and living in peace with her neighbors."

I thought carefully before replying. "They are perceptive questions, and it would take a long time to answer them fully. The history of the Jewish people has always been exciting and complicated. We've influenced the world more often for good, which all too frequently has caused us to be the target of our enemies. You'll know better than most that we've produced outstanding academics, musicians, doctors, lawyers and business entrepreneurs, as well as national and municipal leaders. There's an interesting statistic which shows that Jews, with just 0.2% of the world population, provided more than 125 Nobel Prize winners, a third of them for medicine."

"That is truly impressive and demonstrates the power of good, but has this brought happiness and harmony to Israel and her people?"

I wanted to explain what had happened in the Middle East over the last half a century, how it had affected those who live there, how it affected my life and that of my friends and so many others living in the Diaspora.

"The country has made massive strides since its establishment in 1948. Israel became the 59th member of the United Nations just one year later and is a democracy governed by coalition, the result of the voting system called proportional representation." In answer to a look of some surprise on his face, I explained, "This means that the parliament consists of members of different parties in proportion to the number of votes cast for that party, and not for the individual."

"Yes, I'm aware of the system which has its roots over 200 ago," and adding with a smile, "the man credited by many with inventing the system was a schoolteacher in Birmingham, England, Thomas Wright Hill. What's surprised me is that Israel chose this system, which often leads to unfair influence by extreme minority parties."

I wasn't sure whether or not I was proud of my fellow citizen of Birmingham whose system meant that in Israel just one and a half percent of the population – that is 55,000 voters – can elect a member of the Knesset.

"You're right, and there's a view that because of the voting system, the religious parties in Israel exert far more influence than their support in the country justifies. In Israel's last general election, fifteen parties participated and the largest party, the newly established Kadima, a split from the Likud Party, won twenty-nine seats out of the 120 being contested. Ehud Olmert, the acting leader in place of the stricken Ariel Sharon, spent weeks endeavoring to form a government. This included the Pensioners' Party…"

"The *which* party?" exclaimed Theodor, with a look of total amazement on his face.

I smiled. "The Pensioners' Party won seven seats and I have to admit it may well contribute rather more sense than some of the other parties. For all that, Israel is fully democratic with a quality legal system and all the services you'd expect to find in a civilized modern country. Sadly, one of the drains on the economy has been the need to keep mobilized an effective defense force comprising conscripted young men and women. The country has been at war from the day it declared independence. Eight years later came the Sinai Campaign, then the conflict in June 1967, named the Six Day War. Then again in October 1973, this time named the Yom Kippur War, because of the day on which it started, and yet again in 1982 with the invasion of Lebanon, and since then continual battles and skirmishes. In recent times, Israel has faced thousands of terrorist attacks with a new phenomenon of suicide bombers and the intifada, a civil uprising by the Palestinian Arabs in what has become known in some of the world's media as the 'occupied territories'. Following the Six Day War, with Israel victorious on every front and the City of Jerusalem once again united, there was huge optimism amongst Israelis that perhaps peace was within their grasp. The Arab armies had been totally defeated and there was a feeling that the Arabs would come to the negotiating table, if only to recover their lost territories. Sadly this didn't happen; their defeat and humiliation merely hardened attitudes and Arab opinion."

"You mention this intifada, a word with which I'm not familiar. What caused this uprising?"

"Apparently, Mr. Ariel Sharon, before he became prime minister, made a controversial visit in 2000 to the Temple Mount which, as you know, is the site of the Dome of the Rock and the Aqsa Mosque. He didn't enter the mosque but was escorted by several hundred policemen and during the visit announced that the area would remain for ever under Israeli control."

"Now I begin to understand why the Arabs in Palestine felt humiliated and perhaps provoked into rising up against the Israeli government."

"That may be so, but there was later evidence that this uprising or intifada was planned long before the Sharon visit, and this was merely used as an excuse."

"Sadly, that's the result of mistrust between two peoples and will remain so until there is inspired leadership on both sides – people who can remove the mistrust."

I sensed I was rushing through the story and Theodor would need further clarification. I poured another cup of tea for each of us and offered a cake, as we'd managed to consume most of the sandwiches.

He nodded as he accepted a small éclair and then looked at me with a questioning look. "You've explained about the continual military struggle, which saddens me greatly, and these, suicide attacks, but you've not mentioned the result of these wars. What happened to the boundaries, did peace result, what was the impact on the Arab neighbors, and the Jews, for that matter?"

I wasn't sure how to begin, if we were to leave the relaxing setting of the Savoy Hotel lounge before dinner was served, so I ventured a reply. "What I propose is that I endeavor to explain what happened during this last half a century, and then we'll see if we can return to Jerusalem to discuss the lessons, the impact and perhaps what the future might hold. After all, Theodor, you've dreamed once before, perhaps we might dream together."

"What an admirable suggestion. I concur completely. I'll listen attentively, and then we'll retire and make plans to visit the Holy Land and, as you say, dream together."

I started to explain how the young state had become embroiled in an era of nonstop wars. The War of Independence in 1948 was seen very differently by the opposing combatants. The Jews saw the opening shots as being fired by the invading armies on the day independence was declared. Egypt bombed Tel Aviv, the Iraqi army marched across the border and further attacks came from Jordan, Lebanon and Syria, with the encouragement of the other Arab nations. The local population, joined by young Zionists who rushed to Israel's aid from around the world, were told to build shelters and avoid gathering in large numbers. On the other hand, the Arabs felt the Zionists had mounted a campaign to expel thousands of Arabs by intimidating them into fleeing their homes. This was the root of the refugee problem which has never been resolved, not least by Arab countries that could have solved the issue at a stroke. Despite the obvious vast difference in populations, the Arabs also contended that the Jews were militarily better organized and superior in numbers.

"Perhaps that's just as well, as I find this start to my dream very depressing. Even accepting that the lines of the partition were not ideal, surely it was a new beginning."

"True, but you have to realize that the original borders were impossible to defend, given the avowed determination of all the Arab states to force the Jews into the Mediterranean Sea, a determination still held by some. The Jewish State, which was seventy-five percent desert, was divided into three parts joined in two places by a strip of land just several kilometers wide."

I explained that following various truces, Israel ended up with new enlarged borders, Jordan annexing a large part of the West Bank of the River Jordan, with Egypt taking the Gaza Strip.

"You've not mentioned Jerusalem, cherished by all the peoples of the city. Where did she fit into this complicated, troublesome plan?"

"The City of Jerusalem was internationalized by the United Nations partition plan, divided between Israel and Jordan, and in effect was totally isolated from the rest of the Jewish population. During the War of Independence, the Old City was captured by the Arab Legion and much of the Jewish Quarter was destroyed. Some of the fiercest fighting of the war took place around Jerusalem, surrounded by Arab villages and attacks from the Jordanians in the north and the Egyptians in the south. One of the great chapters of Israeli history is the siege of Jerusalem. The road from Tel Aviv was continually under attack from the overlooking former British police fort at Latrun, and the construction of a track, known as the 'Burma Road' after the road built by British and American forces during Second World War to allow supplies to China, enabled relief to get through to the Jews in Jerusalem. Israel was in possession of Mount Scopus, which included the Hebrew University and Hadassah Hospital and remained isolated from the rest of Israel for nearly twenty years. Jerusalem was declared by Israel as its capital; this proclamation was and remains disputed by the Arabs and the UN. It was not long before Israel found itself at war again and this time the cause was the Suez Canal."

Theodor raised his eyebrows at recognition of the strategic importance of the waterway, and no doubt recalling his own trip along the canal.

"Fifty years ago, in July 1956, Egyptian president Nasser nationalized the Suez Canal, apparently reflecting his unhappiness with the lack of financial support from the Western nations for the building of the Aswan Dam. Within months, following unsuccessful diplomatic negotiations, and the announcement of a united Jordanian, Syrian and Egyptian army, Israel, supported by the French and clearly encouraged by Britain, invaded the Sinai and reached the Suez Canal in just four days. When British and French forces joined the affray, there was worldwide condemnation particularly from the United States and the Soviet Union. Hostilities ended, the Suez Canal was blocked by forty ships, wrecked and sunk to stop international passage, and Britain and France withdrew with their pride and political reputation severely damaged. The British prime minister subsequently resigned, and Israel occupied the Sinai Desert for the next few months."

My story was becoming a sad saga of military conflict, whilst the young state fought an economic battle to survive and absorb the thousands of Jews seeking to establish a new home in the Promised Land. It was only another eleven years before the region's countries were again at war. The early months of 1967 were marked by repeated attacks on settlements in northern Israel by Syria, backed by the Soviet Union. Egypt began massing its forces and announced that United Nations peace- keeping forces stationed on its border with Israel were to be removed. The United

Nations failed to take any preventive action and it was clear that war was brewing. This feeling was intensified when Nasser imposed an illegal blockade on the international waterway, the Straits of Tiran, leading into the Gulf of Aqaba. This effectively blocked the southern access from the open seas to the State of Israel.

A shocked Theodor asked quietly, "Was there no international concern, no diplomatic activity? After all, this was the baby nation conceived by the United Nations with the care of so many 'midwives.'"

"There was considerable activity by the Israeli ambassador to the United States, Avraham Harman, and by Israel's foreign minister, Abba Eban, whose diplomatic skill was matched only by his eloquence with the English language. He flew across the world back and forth, seeking support and a solution to the crisis, but his efforts came to naught. The world's leaders, presidents, prime ministers and diplomats, pontificated and stood and watched. The Israeli nation, not yet twenty years old, feared that, once again, it was in danger of being annihilated." Theodor sat on the edge of his seat as he urged to me to continue. "The Israeli government appointed Moshe Dayan as defense minister, and with future prime minister Yitzhak Rabin as chief of staff, a bold plan was agreed. On the morning of June 5, 1967, Israel launched a pre-emptive strike on the airfields of Egypt, Syria and Jordan and destroyed 400 aircraft still on the ground, rendering their enemies incapable of striking back. The war lasted just six days, hence its name. Israel had captured the West Bank and the Gaza Strip, reached the Suez Canal, occupied Sharm e-Sheikh and the Golan Heights, and most important of all, Jerusalem was once again a united Jewish city."

As I paused, Theodor raised both his hands before speaking. "I'd like to think that this dramatic military victory would somehow bring a peaceful outcome, but experience has taught me that wounded nations – just like people – will not forgive easily, particularly when the result is loss of land accompanied by loss of reputation and status."

"True, I'm afraid. A further 200,000 Arab refugees were created, welcomed neither in their former homeland nor in their Arab host countries. But it was the impact of the Israeli General Mordechai Gur entering the Old City through the Lions Gate, capturing the Dome of the Rock and leading Dayan and Rabin to the Western Wall of the ancient Temple of King Solomon that set every pair of Jewish eyes throughout the world crying with sheer emotion. The Jewish people had returned to their biblical home, and the feeling of security from the amazing and speedy military victory was temporarily pushed from their minds. I suppose these six days were to set the scene for the next four decades. The Israeli people enjoyed a new self-confidence and, despite many calls from some countries for Israel to withdraw from the territories they occupied, there was also a new respect for this small nation which had conquered the combined might of the Arab enemy.

"This great victory sadly didn't bring peace. The following years were dominated by bomb explosions in Tel Aviv and Jerusalem, and continued spasmodic fighting on the borders, despite the arrival of United Nations observers. In 1968 yet another new form of attack on civilians appeared when an El Al passenger plane flying to Rome was hijacked by Arab terrorists, the only such successful attempt against an Israeli aircraft."

I could see a strange look come over his face as I realized that my language may not have been fully understood. "You may recall that in the December 1903, when you were so ill, the Wright Brothers made their first flight in a flying machine. That machine flew only 120 feet, achieving an altitude of ten feet for just twelve seconds, but it demonstrated the belief of Wilbur Wright – which he shared with the French aviation pioneer Octave Chanute – that 'flight is possible to man'. This event signaled the start of a significant change in the way man traveled the world and, sadly, how such a wonderful invention could be misused by those determined to be evil. Today you can fly by airplane from Vienna to New York without a stop in less than nine hours.

"While there had been a hijacking ten years earlier in Cuba, it was the attempt in 1970 by Palestinian Arabs to hijack four planes simultaneously and land them in the Jordanian desert which attracted worldwide attention. They were successful, with three planes blown up on the ground after the hostages were freed. They failed with the fourth El Al plane."

It was clear that some explanation about hijacking was necessary, as Theodor looked at me, somewhat confused. When I felt that he understood, I decided to tell him about one of the most daring escapades in Israel's history. "In June 1976, four terrorists, two fighting for the liberation of Palestine and two from the German Baader-Meinhof gang, seized an Air France plane with 250 people on board and diverted it to Entebbe, Uganda. After demands for the release of prisoners held in Israeli and other prisons, Ugandan president Idi Amin offered his support for the hijackers and their aims. But it was the decision to free most of the passengers except for the Jews and Israelis that caused alarm. The Israeli government decided any separation policy – which had been the hallmark of the Nazis – was totally unacceptable, and that they had to take immediate action. An elite force was dispatched on the 2,500-mile journey from Tel Aviv to Entebbe, and a surprise attack was made on the terminal building. The dangerous mission was a complete success, although the leader of the mission was killed. The hostages, including the Air France crew who had stayed voluntarily with their passengers, were freed and returned to Israel to the relief of their families and Jewish people throughout the world."

"Amazing, but isn't it merely a new generation of piracy?" came the retort. "I think I can understand the concept of what you're telling me, but it is so terribly sad, having once considered Uganda as a haven for the Jewish people."

I thought that as the day was drawing to a close I would tell Theodor about the Yom Kippur War, after which it was probably time to give him a rest, and talk about our return to the location of his vision and dream.

"Yom Kippur 1973 was a Day of Atonement which will live long in Jewish memories all over the world, in Israel but also throughout the Diaspora. On October 3, two days before the start of the most solemn day in the Jewish calendar, reports were coming in of unusual movements by the Soviet-armed Syrian and Egyptian armies. There was no feeling of urgency and two of Israel's finest generals, Moshe Dayan and Yigal Allon, were advising prime minister Golda Meir that there was no cause for immediate concern. However, when news that the Soviet Union was evacuating its advisers from Syria, the air force was placed on alert and Israeli forces moved to the Golan Heights. Israeli intelligence, the envy of the world, had failed to identify the signs or perhaps the chief of staff failed to translate them into the action needed, and it looked as if the country, for the first time, would be caught totally by surprise."

Theodor shook his head. "Most of the world will be aware that Yom Kippur is the day when almost all Jews, including those like me who aren't religious, attend synagogue to join their fellow Jews in a time of reflection and hope for the coming year. I still recall the haunting and solemn melody of the *Kol Nidre* prayer sung so movingly by our *chazan*, beginning the fast on the previous evening. So, I can identify with the threat of surprise about which you speak."

"I can tell you that on the morning of October 6 – Yom Kippur – an unprecedented event was in progress. As they prayed in the synagogues, military reserves were receiving their orders to return to their units immediately and sirens began wailing in every city and settlement. Because of the holy day, the whole of Israel was at a standstill, radio stations were closed and so news was based only on rumor and word of mouth. In the early afternoon, the radio came alive, sirens started again and the nation was ordered to the shelters. Israel was under attack on its northern border on the Golan Heights, and in the south where the Egyptians had crossed the Suez Canal into Sinai. During the first couple of days of hostilities, things went very badly for Israel with the Syrians marching down from the Golan. As the conflict progressed, Israel turned the odds and by October 26, when a truce was agreed, the Israeli army was within forty kilometers of Damascus and had crossed the Suez Canal, cutting off and surrounding an entire Egyptian army."

"Perhaps I don't understand. Even with limited knowledge, why didn't Israel make a pre-emptive strike as it did in 1967? And may I presume that once again the world powers stood and watched?"

"The Middle East conflict was at the center of world politics, with Moscow providing military and financial support for the Arabs, and Washington giving help to the Israelis. In many ways Palestine was but a pawn in a struggle between the two great world powers vying for domination. The Israeli high command recommended a pre-emptive strike, but Golda Meir, who had clear political antennae, decided that to keep the United States on its side it was essential that, despite the threat, Israel shouldn't start the war. She was fully aware of the economic threat to the West by an Arab oil embargo, and the mixture of intrigue was intensified by President Nixon's distraction with the Watergate scandal which was to prompt his resignation ten months later."

Theodor sat back in the comfortable chair, took a sip of tea, which by now must have been cold, sighed deeply and said, "You've given me an excellent commentary on the first thirty years of Israel's life. I want to hear more about your exploits and those of your generation and I can think of no better location for you to share those memories than in Jerusalem."

With that instruction – for it couldn't be interpreted any other way – I called for the bill, we rose and left the elegant surroundings of the Savoy.

CHAPTER NINETEEN

Jerusalem, Israel, 2006

It was Friday evening and the warm sun was beginning to hide behind the Citadel as its final rays reflected the gold of the Dome of the Rock. I was strolling with Theodor and beginning a walk through the pages of the Bible, as we speculated about the history of the Jewish people and the turbulent relationships with their neighbors throughout the generations. We'd entered the Old City of Jerusalem, through the Zion Gate, which had borne the onslaught of thousands of years of military attacks and still bears the scars of the 1948 War of Independence. The Gate provides access to two of the Old City's quarters, the Armenian and Jewish. We were making our way to the Western Wall, which is the central point for Jews – religious and secular – to welcome the Sabbath. As we walked through what a few hours earlier had been bustling narrow streets and alleys we were captivated by the lingering smells of spices and sweetmeats, and a glance through gaps in the shutters of exotic displays of colorful fruit and vegetables. This is the Middle East for "real," as final bartering between trader and tourist over a trinket or souvenir is witnessed outside some of the small shops and stalls as they begin to close for the Sabbath.

Earlier in the day, and not far from where we walk, Franciscan monks had led Christian pilgrims along the Via Dolorosa towards the Church of the Holy Sepulchre, retracing the struggling steps of Jesus, a heavy cross on his shoulders. His wearisome journey would have made a strong contrast with those of the pilgrims, as they were coaxed and tempted by traders and merchants seeking to sell their wares.

We stood on the path leading to the Temple Mount overlooking the scene of the large square in front of the Western Wall. The Temple Mount – the place where the Old and the New Testaments come together – is where Abraham prepared his son Isaac for sacrifice and where King Solomon built the First Temple. After its destruction it became the site of the Second Temple and now the only reminder still standing is the Western Wall. It is cherished too by Christians, who associate the Temple Mount with the preaching of Jesus, as well as by Muslims who believe it to be where Muhammad began his ascent to heaven. Where else in our troubled world can you hear the competing sounds of the muezzin's call to the mosque, the pealing of church bells and the voice of the *chazan*, praying in the synagogue.

As we gazed upon this historic site, Theodor lifted his hands as if struck by some majestic sign. "This is truly the miracle about which I dreamed, the return of the Jewish people to their birthplace. I can see from their dress and appearance that people from all over the world have assembled here to celebrate the Sabbath and the re-dedication of a nation."

We stood silently for some time before he spoke again. "I can recognize the clothes of the bearded Orthodox Jews with their locks of hair falling to their shoulders and traditional black hats, but what of the young men and women with the faded trousers and shirts clearly inside out?"

I was puzzled for just a moment before replying with a laugh, "Those are clearly tourists from either the United States, England or even France and that's what's called 'fashion', and now followed as much by young men as young women." With that, I went on to explain that the dull blue trousers were jeans brought to the civilized world from the wild west of America, originally by Levi

Strauss, and worn so often with a T-shirt emblazoned with the name of the designer or some political statement. From his expression I gathered he found our generation somewhat strange.

"Let's go down to the Wall and spend a few moments listening and joining in the Sabbath prayers and you'll see that there's a tradition of placing a message, or prayer, in between the stones of the Wall." As we approached the growing crowd, he asked about the dividing fence between the men and women. When the Temple was built (in biblical times), within a narrow thoroughfare, it wasn't divided. "As this is now regarded as a place of prayer, Orthodox Jewish law requires that men and women should pray separately." He nodded in understanding, without indicating his approval.

It had become dark with a slight chill in the air and we decided to walk back to our hotel. "We've much to talk about before the Sabbath is out. I want to hear about how you and your generation reacted to those early traumatic years of Israel's statehood."

We were sitting comfortably in the hotel lounge as we watched the other guests, dressed more sedately than at the Wall. The men, in crisp white shirts and dark trousers, sat with children, who had fallen uncharacteristically silent, with their wives and mothers in neat dresses. In a country which had continued to be at war for over half a century it seemed to me to be a brief oasis of spiritual tranquillity, and quite unique to Jerusalem.

"We talked, Theodor, about my first visit to Israel in 1956. I suppose in many ways this experience was to change my life. After my friend Leo Cohen and I returned to England, we threw ourselves totally into the work of the Jewish National Fund." This clearly received the total approval of Theodor, who recalled the establishment of the Fund in 1901 when he prophesied that it would become the foundation of the establishment of the National Home.

"We devoted our efforts to raising funds through the organization of innovative events, first in our home city of Birmingham, and then beyond as we helped to establish the National Younger

JNF movement which, to this day, has captured the imagination of so many generations of young Jews living outside Israel. It was not just a fund-raising machine; it was a social and cultural experience. I recall the outstanding leadership qualities of the likes of Sir Trevor Chinn, Cyril Stein and Conrad Morris, whose contribution to Israel's welfare was inspirational. We followed the news of the young state's progress, and then I visited Israel again, this time with my wife, in November 1963."

I stopped momentarily to explain about the assassination of American president John F. Kennedy and how you always remember "where you were" on such historic occasions. I was in Tel Aviv on November 22, 1963, and witnessed the horror and emotion of the whole of the world to this tragedy.

"It was the Six Day War which mobilized the effort, as well as the passion of Jews across the world, not least of all in Birmingham. As we listened to the news bulletins describing the Israeli air strike, in response to the threat of an Arab invasion, we stopped work and rushed to our community office. There were two objectives, first to raise funds to ensure that the economic and welfare life of the country continued, and to encourage young people to go to Israel to work on the kibbutzim to relieve those who'd gone to war. My role was to interview and screen the volunteers who wished to work in the fields, and I'm proud to say that my younger brother, Derek, was among the first to leave. He went to Kibbutz Afikim in the Jordan Valley just below Lake Kinneret, in the shadow of the Golan Heights, and I believe the experience, shared with so many others, has stayed with them all their lives."

"How did you feel living so far away when Israel was under threat? Didn't you want to leave the safety and comfort of Great Britain – however tolerant the society – and go to live among the Jewish people in their homeland? You could have gone without being forced to go or without fear of the experiences of the Jewish communities in Europe."

I didn't know how to begin to answer. These were searching questions and went to the heart of the meaning of Zionism.

Could one be a Zionist and continue to live in the Diaspora? So many members of our community had gone on aliya and whilst the thought had occurred to me on a number of occasions, I either lacked the courage or was content with my life amongst family and community.

"Those are questions I often ask myself. The answers I find are excuses rather than reasons – the family business, family responsibilities, community commitment. But within that commitment I feel that I've met a range of obligations. Service to my own community and city brings huge rewards and satisfaction, thirty years as a Birmingham city councillor, becoming only the fourth member of the Jewish community to be elected lord mayor, and serving as president of the Birmingham Hebrew Congregation."

Theodor interrupted me to question. "And what about your Zionist commitment?"

I didn't give a direct answer. "It was again the time when Israel found herself under threat, in October 1973, that the Jewish people rose up in support and to rush to her aid. The Arabs felt that there'd been no political progress in resolving the issue of the lost territories in the earlier wars, and frustration about this and the growing refugee problem had spread throughout the Arab World. There was widespread mistrust of each other by both sides to the conflict and for all of these reasons the Arabs felt totally justified in going to war with Israel. I was in Singers Hill Synagogue with family and friends as the *Ne'ila* service – closing prayers – of Yom Kippur were bringing the solemn and tiring fast day to a close. Someone rushed into the synagogue and spoke to our rabbi, who came to the pulpit to announce that the BBC's correspondent in Israel, Michael Elkins, was reporting that the Syrians had invaded Israel across the Golan Heights and the Egyptian army was on the move across the Sinai. The whole of the synagogue fell silent as the thoughts of those present raced across the distance to think about the plight of loved ones living there. It appeared that Israel, possibly for the first time, had been caught off guard. The immediate impact was unparalleled. Despite the twenty-five hour fast, food and drink disappeared from our minds and we met that evening to plan how we could support Israel in what appeared to be the biggest threat since her establishment."

Theodor took a sip from his glass and I joined him as my memory raced back to the closing minutes of that Yom Kippur fast day. "And so how were you involved with the support on this occasion?"

"There was a huge national campaign to raise funds so that, once again, the economic life of Israel could continue. I was appointed to the national committee and given the brief, jointly with Alan Millett in London, to mobilize the support of all the Jewish communities, large and small, throughout the United Kingdom. We traveled up and down the country, meeting and speaking with groups as large as several hundred in Glasgow, Liverpool and Bournemouth, to others in the remote parts of the country, with just a mere handful, but all equally enthusiastic to support. I suppose if I'm truthful, the most traumatic experiences were the repeated visits to Israel leading groups of well-wishers and supporters so that they could witness at first hand the hard times being experienced by the battle-weary Israelis."

My mind went back to those heady days of winter 1973 when our lives seemed dominated by the daily news from the Middle East. I told Theodor how we were called to London for briefings, often at short notice. We met in Baker Street, in the offices of Marks and Spencer under the watchful eyes of the founders of that great business, the Lords Simon Marks, Israel and Marcus Sieff, and led by Michael Sacher – all great Jewish benefactors and outstanding Zionists. I recall receiving a summons to breakfast in London's Churchill Hotel when all we were told was that the guest was very special. Security was intense, and imagine our surprise when Golda Meir, Israel's legendary prime minister, walked into the room to a thunderous ovation. She addressed us quietly, authoritatively and more in the tones of a 75-year-old grandmother than a 75-year-old prime minister. She spoke of the opening battles in the Sinai when huge numbers of Egyptian infantry, just like a plague of locusts in the sand, were sent to surround the Israeli tanks and died unprotected on the spot. She spoke with total emotion of the huge price in human life paid by Israel for the decision on the morning of Yom Kippur not to attack first so that the "world would not accuse us". We left, most of us with tears in our eyes, all of us enthralled and inspired, and without eating breakfast!

"Theodor, these were times when one felt part of history. There were so many other memorable occasions. Lunch in Jerusalem with former general Yigael Yadin, the military leader and archeologist whose research into the Dead Sea Scrolls made him world famous; a tour of the Sinai on a military bus guided by Chaim Topol, an actor who played the lead in the musical *Fiddler on the Roof* in London's West End. One of the most moving experiences was carrying from our synagogue in Birmingham a Torah scroll, and watching close friend Ivor Lewis hand it over for use by a military group serving on the Golan Heights. And there was a tough challenge to face too. England, with France, had introduced an arms embargo which prevented Israel from obtaining urgently needed spare parts for their British supplied tanks. Efforts in London to reach Lord Carrington, the defense secretary and chairman of the Conservative Party, had failed. I discovered that he was due in Birmingham on October 20 for a Conservative Dinner, and I seized the opportunity to meet him privately with a colleague, the Rev. Sidney Gold."

Theodor looked at me. "I hope your discussion proved more successful than some of those I had with government leaders who displayed understanding and sympathy, but very little else."

My answer wouldn't surprise him. "We expressed deep concern that whilst the government had been quick to condemn Israel, they had failed to condemn the Arab aggression. With the limited time at our disposal we then asked him to use his considerable influence to remove the arms embargo, as he was one of prime minister Edward Heath's most trusted advisers. He sought to reassure us that the government was fully aware of the situation, was equally anxious to ensure that Israel's security was preserved and that specific spare parts would not be delayed. Within the thirty minutes at our disposal we had to be content with words of comfort. The war came to an end six days after our meeting."

"What was happening in the old homes of the Jews, in Poland and in Russia? It was these people for whom I intended the Jewish State to be established, for I cannot believe that, even with the passage of time, their lives were any happier than in previous times."

"Correct. Your plan to accept the Uganda option for a Jewish National Home arose out of your deep concern following the Kishinev pogrom. Russian Jews had always been subject to waves of anti-Semitism from the time of the czars, through Hitler's invasion, and this continued under the rule of Stalin. Despite allowing the hundred or so minorities living in the Soviet Union to practice their own religion, culture and tradition, this was denied to the Jews, who continued to be oppressed and deprived of opportunity, both in employment as well as worship."

Theodor nodded in understanding. "And what was the attitude of Jews in the rest of the world?"

"A window of opportunity began to open. Mikhail Gorbachev came to power as leader of the Communist Party and introduced reforms that opened up the Soviet Union to economic restructuring in a period termed perestroika. The West, particularly the United States and Britain, seized on the opportunity, named glasnost, as a period of more open debate, relaxation of censorship and freedom of speech as well as freeing the people from the stranglehold of government control and hence the ability to travel. This did not, however, immediately apply to the Jews of Russia, many of whom wished to emigrate to Israel, and not only was this denied but families were separated as oppression continued. There was also a rise in nationalism creating tensions amongst the people, and whilst thousands of dissidents and political prisoners were released, you'll not be surprised to learn that Jews weren't included. It was to be another few years, in 1991, when the iron curtain between East and West was flung open and the Soviet Union was finally broken up."

I wanted to tell Herzl of two experiences in my life when I came into close contact with Russia, the country of my own heritage. Jews were isolated, imprisoned, because they were Jews. The only contact many had with the outside world was infrequent, they were monitored and their phone calls tapped. One such Soviet Jew was Anatoly (later Natan) Sharansky, and I was his contact. Sharansky later emigrated to Israel and rose to become a government minister. Could there be a better example of hope and redemption?

In 1988 I was given the unique experience to visit Moscow. The main purpose was to identify some works of art – Russian icons and other artifacts never before seen outside the Soviet Union – to bring to Birmingham for an exhibition. This was aimed at opening up the relationship between our city, its people and its business, with the expanding Russian economy. Fortunately for the world of culture, I was in the company of an expert from the city's Art Gallery and also Councillor [later Sir] Richard Knowles, the Labor leader of the City Council and a good friend of Israel, whose knowledge of icons was probably not much better than mine.

Our arrival on a Friday afternoon only confirmed some of the preconceived ideas I had of the Soviet Union of that time. We were met by officials, driven in an official car to a hotel accommodating official guests. Even allowing for the impact of Red Square, the Kremlin and St Basil's Cathedral and watching the Changing of the Guard, dating from the time of Peter the Great, I found the city miserable – just like many of the buildings, the people and the weather. But the subway was spotless and efficient, the walls free of graffiti and I was told, the streets safe to walk about and few, if any, muggings. There were queues everywhere as people joined the line, at times not knowing why they did so. It was just part of the Soviet culture.

I had an additional objective to my brief visit. Despite being under the constant watch of the Soviet security police, I managed to slip away to make a phone call from a public call box having been warned that under no circumstances was I to phone from my room. I was trying to reach one of a number of Jewish "refuse-niks", whose efforts to obtain exit visas had been refused, to bring them news of the outside world and of Israel. Having arranged to meet my contact in the street at a precise time, I left my hotel and walked in the cold night along the street, and coming towards me was a short, well-built man with coat, turned-up collar and peaked cap. Neither of us seemed to hesitate as our eyes met in instant recognition. We clasped hands and with a warm smile, he greeted me with the traditional Sabbath greeting, "Shabbat Shalom". Binyamin Charney, who looked a decade older than his 47 years, took my arm and conducted me through the dark side streets to his second-floor apartment on Bryanskaya Street where we were greeted by his wife, Yadviga, and some friendly neighbors.

Despite some language difficulties, we managed to talk as we shared the bread and wine of the Sabbath table. We spoke of the imminent arrival of the festival of Passover, the traditional time of the exodus of the children of Israel from Egyptian oppression. I couldn't stay long, having been warned not to be on the streets late in the evening, and as I offered some gifts from England, I left this warm and hospitable Jewish family who yearned for the freedom which I enjoyed and the opportunity to be reunited with their people. This experience had a considerable impact on me as I realized how we Jews are bound together by our belief in the State of Israel, regardless of the barrier of language and geography.

"You've certainly witnessed historic changes in the times of the Jewish people, and I applaud what your generation's achieved. You've certainly succeeded where, perhaps, I failed."

"My dear Theodor, on the contrary, you inspired not just my generation but every generation who followed you. It was your vision of a Jewish National Home, your tireless efforts in so many European capitals and your challenge, which was never allowed to disappear, which motivated thousands of Zionists to work towards achieving your goal. The creation of the State of Israel reflected in this unique city of Jerusalem, in which we now sit, is not just a tribute to you but the result of your inspiration and drive. Today you should not speak of failure but pride and success."

"I hear all you say and I've enjoyed listening to the story of the first half century of Israel's life, and now I pose a question. What about the future? From all I hear, I fear that if we were sitting here in another fifty years' time, there would still be conflict and mistrust. The combination of Jewish obstinacy and the huge might of the Arab people does not augur well for a peaceful solution, but we must find an answer. Too many young people have given their lives, too many families are bereaved – a Jewish child has the same value as an Arab child to the parents who brought them into the world. For the sake of the generation which is growing up there must be hope that they can live in peace with their neighbors who have, after all, descended from the same father. I feel that if these two great peoples *combined* their talents, rather than fought over them, they would be a force for good which would lead the world."

I listened to Theodor Herzl's words, and I looked at him with admiration and wondered if, just if, his inspiration and dream could somehow be revitalized to find a formula for the peace which had escaped so many. It was certainly worth asking, and I set myself the objective to challenge him when next we met.

CHAPTER TWENTY

Vienna, Austria, 2006

I have had a remarkable experience. Some readers may feel that my imagination has rather run away with itself as I set out on a journey to meet one of the giants of Jewish history. Theodor Herzl died at forty-four, exhausted and sick from racing around Europe trying to influence some of the most important government and religious leaders of his time. He met with the German kaiser, the pope and the British prime minister, and his impact on the Zionist cause was huge, despite being limited to barely ten years. Is he forgotten today by young Jews, comfortable and assimilated into Western societies, or merely regarded as a bearded European, looking much older than his years, and gazing out over an anonymous balcony?

He saw himself as a failure, but we know that his dream became a reality forty-four years after his death. Within the pages of this book I have tried to re-kindle the dreams of bygone generations so that those who follow can more easily understand the emotions of our parents and grandparents, feel the excitement of the Zionist dream and know that the reborn State of Israel can and should be a force for good, as well as an influence for peace in an unstable region.

So I had returned to Vienna where my journey began. I was heading for the Sacher Hotel in the Kärntner Strasse. I could not think of a more appropriate location outside Israel to have my final meeting with Herzl than this great historic hotel in the city where we first met. I sat by the window of the lounge, whose walls have witnessed so much conversation and debate around the politics and culture of Europe, and looked out on the square dominated by the grandiose Opera House as I waited for my guest to arrive.

I didn't have to wait too long. Theodor Herzl entered the lounge, and seeing me stand up to greet him, walked quickly to the table, grasped my hand and with a warm greeting, sat opposite.

"It's good to see you again, and I trust I find you in good spirits. We've spent many hours discussing what's gone before, in my time and in yours. *But what about the future?* I spent nine years, at times it seemed like two or three times as long, speaking, writing, dreaming and meeting with some of Europe's great leaders. I was exhausted at the end, and what did I achieve? You speak of the inspiration I left with those that followed me and to know that my vision of a Jewish homeland came to be some four decades later fills me with pride and satisfaction. But what now? Over a century has elapsed since the first Zionist Congress in Basel, and for all the good achieved by both our generations, Israel is not a land of just milk and honey, for there is too much blood running down the streets of Tel Aviv and Jerusalem, as well as of Gaza and Ramallah."

Some coffee and cakes arrived, served with a style which spanned our generations. I was anxious to encourage Theodor to keep talking because he might just have the formula, perhaps another dream, from which could be built the foundation to bring together the warring sides.

I posed an opening question. "Let's begin by examining this strange country called Palestine –where did it come from, how was it inhabited, who, if anyone has a claim of sovereignty?"

"It was the Romans who initially gave the name Palaestina, presumably after the Philistines, to part of Syria, with the objective of erasing any form of Jewish identity. There have been Jews living in the country for nearly 4,000 years, even though the numbers fluctuated widely and they almost disappeared at the time of the Crusades. The Jewish population grew again under Ottoman rule to some 45,000 but was outnumbered by the half a million or so Arabs. The land was described, first by the British Consul in 1857 as 'empty of inhabitants', and a few years later by the author Mark Twain as 'desolate and unlovely'. Turning to your times, what would you say is the population of Israel today?"

"It would be around seven million; three quarters of those are Jewish with another seven million Jews in the rest of the world. Indeed, over five million live in the United States alone."

"That's remarkable. When we held the first Zionist Congress in 1897, a similar number lived in Russia and Poland, and whilst estimates were unclear, I suppose there were around eleven million Jews worldwide. It was always clear to me that there would be widespread Arab opposition to Jewish settlement and I felt strongly that we should encourage the Arabs to live amongst their own people."

"Are you saying that you wished to remove the Arabs from Palestine altogether?" I asked, with some amazement.

"No, not in the way you speak. The Arabs deserved exactly the same hope as the Jews. My plan was to resettle them with full compensation and help so that they'd have homes and the opportunity to work the land for the benefit of their families."

I looked at Theodor as I was unsure how such a proposal would ever work or be accepted by the Palestinian Arabs.

"I'm not sure that Palestine was ever really an Arab country," I suggested. "Arab leaders themselves have claimed that there was no Palestine in the Bible and it was a Zionist invention. There was certainly no mention of Palestine or Palestinian refugees in Resolution 242 of the United Nations which called for Israel to withdraw to the pre-1967 borders. And just as important, all of the organizations with Palestine in their names, such as *The Palestine Post*, the Palestine Symphony Orchestra, even the Joint Palestine

191

Appeal, were all Jewish organizations. Until 1948 and even beyond, Palestinian mainly described Jews."

"That may be the Jewish view, but does it reflect the Palestinian Arab view?" Theodor interjected.

"Probably not, but the facts support it, and the two sides have become polarized. With the election of two strong characters to the leadership of Israel and what has become known as the Palestinian Authority – Ariel Sharon and Yasser Arafat – negotiations to secure a lasting peace stalled for some time. Accusation and counter-accusation only served to unite the two peoples behind their leaders even if there were groups, Arab and Jewish, who sought a peaceful coexistence. There was simply no trust."

"Not a new situation, and I suspect little progress can be made whilst the two leaders you mention remain in their roles."

I sought to assure Theodor of what had happened. "Arafat died in November 2004. He was the global image of the Palestinian movement; he was, in his own words, 'the inventor of hijacking of passenger planes'. He often spoke in one tone in the Western world, of peace and tolerance, condemning terrorism, and in another in the Middle East, much more belligerent, urging his followers to commit murder. Even more significant, he became wealthy as a result of the financial support intended for the Palestinian Arabs living in poverty. And then, as if some strange and unnatural hand was at work, Sharon was felled by a stroke which removed him completely from the political stage. Here was a man respected, as much as hated, by the Arabs. His career was dominated by a reversal in character from being totally intransigent and the prime mover to settling the occupied territories, to a peace-seeking statesman who withdrew 8,000 settlers from Jewish settlements in the Gaza strip after thirty-eight years."

"How was that proposal received amongst the peoples involved?"

"Moderate Arabs welcomed the move, seeing it as a positive sign in the quest for peace, whilst others rejected the process as insufficient and too late. Israelis were equally divided. Those who lived in the areas being evacuated were clearly enraged and were supported by religious groups, who always believed that Israel was in these territories by biblical right. However, the majority of Jews felt that this provided an opportunity to develop a meaningful relationship with their Arab neighbors, as well as likely to receive the support of the rest of the world. They agreed with Ariel Sharon that such a withdrawal would be painful and risky, but one which offered a ray of hope. It was inconceivable that one million Arab refugees, doubling with every generation, could be confined in camps in poverty and squalor without the hatred growing and growing. This is a people let down by their own leaders and forgotten by their Arab brethren."

Theodor threw up his hands in consternation. "You tell a tale of total despair. It occurs to me that the course of history and with that – the fate of the entire Middle East – lay in the hands of these two men. The destiny of the world has so often rested with men of strong character whose vision at times has been misplaced at best or dangerous at worst. I recall how difficult it was for me to gain the support of some of the most outstanding leaders of Jewry who for one reason or another wouldn't attend the first Zionist Congress. I remember particularly two great rabbis, Zadoc Kahn, chief rabbi of France, and Moritz Güdemann of Vienna, and from your own country, Colonel Goldsmid, for whom I had such respect, and Sir Samuel Montagu, who all pulled out of attending. A great disappointment at the time, particularly as Montagu, a Member of Parliament, claimed to want to settle with his family in Palestine. I was always aware of the comfort in which wealthy Jews felt they lived in the countries of their birth, believing themselves protected from the threat of anti-Semitism. This made me angry for I saw anti-Semitism for what it was and understood its threat. I recognized that however comfortable they felt, Jews would always be seen as strangers, however hard they might try to assimilate."

He smiled as he continued. "We're not good at assimilating. Some of us mix well and play a full role in every aspect of life, but we cannot exchange our identity as Jews for the identity of being British or French or even American. Your generation has been blessed with quality of life, and a complacency of living amongst friendly nations which has been denied to so many Jews of earlier periods. No one knows better than I about assimilation amongst neighbors. I too found it comforting and a temptation not to get involved in the affairs of our people."

I wanted to move on but wished to press him further about anti-Semitism. "What would you say if I told you that in this time of Israel's rebirth there are some who claim to be anti-Zionist but not anti-Semitic?"

"There's no distinction, however hard they try to justify it. Throughout history we've been the subject of hate wherever we've lived, and I suggest to you that Israel and the Jewish people are one and you cannot divide them. The sooner the Jews of your generation recognize that fact, the sooner they will realize that they cannot resign from being Jewish and adopt another identity. That's why I was so determined to see the establishment of a Jewish National Home. I hoped it would put an end to anti-Semitism, but from what you say, I was wrong, yet I remain convinced that its existence will help preserve our people as a nation with the respect of the world."

It was this last statement that spurred me to want to move on to the future, and not dwell on the past.

I reflected on some views of an Arab, who described himself as a moderate, whom I met in Israel. He felt that the best ambassadors for Israel are satisfied Arabs – first her own citizens, then those in Arab society. He believed that the vast majority of Arabs and Jews wanted and yearned for peace, and he was critical of the leadership, both Jewish and Palestinian, all of whom had failed to deliver what they'd promised. There was a need to break the mold and give support to moderate Arab voices. He admitted his shame that the Palestinian Arab refugees had been used by the wealthy Arab countries as political pawns, and was angry that three generations of Arab society had been completely destroyed.

We discussed the 600,000 Jewish refugees who'd been absorbed from Arab countries, and how the world had ignored the impact of the assimilation into the life of this small land of all these immigrants with their cultural, language and economic differences.

With a shrug of his shoulders, Theodor said, "Life is never perfect and there can be no perfect solution. But that doesn't mean we shouldn't seek a solution. Where do we go from here, what does the future hold for the Jewish people as well as for the Palestinian Arabs? You tell me about decades of war, about lack of trust between leaders which only encourages those who follow to prolong and preserve the mistrust. I listen to you speak of the great powers, of presidents, prime ministers and senior diplomats seeking for generations to find a basis of peace and all coming to nothing. And now you speak of a wall being built to divide these two peoples to protect them one from another, from the attacks of these suicide bombers, and I wonder what, if anything, that will solve. For centuries, Jews have lived in ghettos, sometimes self-imposed, at other times imposed by others, and, I have to say, it's a state of mind that encourages us to protect ourselves behind some form of barrier. I speculate as to what my peer, Sigmund Freud, would have made of all of this." He stopped to think and stroked his beard, speaking in a hushed voice I had to strain to hear. "At some stage we have to learn to live with our neighbors. We have to find an understanding of each other and that'll take truly inspirational leadership, Jewish as well as Arab."

I thought I should make Theodor aware of some more recent events as I spoke. "There're a number of critical events which have occurred in recent times which have impacted on the quest for peace. In September 2001 the United States suffered a series of coordinated terrorist attacks. It may be difficult for you to fully understand what I'm about to tell you."

"Why not try?" came the quick reply.

"On Tuesday morning, September 11, 2001, four airplanes carrying a large number of passengers were hijacked. Two were purposely crashed into two tower skyscraper buildings called the World Trade Center, in the center of New York, causing the buildings to collapse and killing all those on board the planes. At about the same time a third plane was hijacked and crashed into the Pentagon in Washington DC, the military headquarters of the United States. A fourth plane crashed into a field in the State of Pennsylvania after a failed attempt by passengers to regain control from the hijackers. Some 3,000 people died in these disasters.

"Let me explain about a skyscraper. This is a very tall building, the first of which was built in America in the late 1880s, and by the time we had advanced to the twentieth century, buildings like the Twin Towers rose into the sky 110 stories high."

While I heard a quiet gasp of surprise, I continued. "As if this weren't enough, four years later, on July 7, 2005, in the middle of the morning rush hour, England's capital, London, was struck by a series of suicide bombs which killed 56 innocent people."

"Who was accused of such a heinous act?"

"The finger was immediately pointed at an Islamic fundamentalist terrorist group called al-Qaeda whose leader, Osama bin Laden, had called for a 'holy war' against the United States and the Jews. He was hero-worshipped by young people throughout the Arab world. These two events completely changed the attitude of the Western powers and especially the United States, who'd never before been subjected to an attack on their own mainland. The British people were of course shocked as well, but had experienced attacks from the air sixty years previously in the Second World War. Then the world became a much more dangerous place when in 2003 Iraq was attacked by a coalition force led by America and Britain and which deposed the tyrannical leader Saddam Hussein. This war was destined to continue for years, amidst world wide doubt and opposition."

"I'm beginning to understand the huge challenges facing your generation. It seems to me the whole world is being divided between the cultures of East and West, the influence of Islam and I suspect the total misuse of the Holy Scriptures – be it the Testaments or the Holy Koran – to generate hate and anger amongst young people. Against this background it's difficult to see how a peace settlement can be achieved in the Holy Land."

"Maybe so, but it was David Ben-Gurion, Israel's first prime minister and one of the architects of the country, who said, 'Despair leads nowhere. Throughout the millennia of persecution, the Jews have realized this and never lost conviction in ultimate justice, peace, and human equality. I'm sure that the Jewish people have hard days ahead of them and overwhelmingly difficult tasks to accomplish but I've total confidence in their ability to pass through the shadows and emerge unshaken, present in the land they have struggled so hard and suffered so greatly to regain.'"

"Those are fine words, and we Jews should never fall into the trap of believing we're the only people to suffer persecution or who have had to struggle to build a homeland. Surely, peace is an objective which is as important to Muslims as it is to Jews and Christians. Those who believe in and follow the Koran will know that the word "peace" is mentioned in it no fewer than fifty-eight times. It is believed to be the most sought-after condition for the life of every human being. So what I have to say to you, my friend, is that there is no alternative for both Jew and Muslim, Israeli and Arab, but to strive for peace. It's an aim which, according to the teachings of Islam, our lives must contain some sort of peace and tranquillity. It will not be achieved lightly, nor without enormous pain. From what you tell me, there's already been too much pain for both peoples, so let us take some refreshment, perhaps a rest and then address our minds to that which so often avoids mankind – *the conquest of peace.*"

We had engaged in a heavy exchange, and whilst I had tried to bring Herzl up to date with events which had such a traumatic impact on my generation, he had seemed to grasp quickly the challenges, understood the problems, and I just wondered if he had the ability to provide even the germ of an idea which could bring about what he had quoted from the teachings of the Koran, "some sort of peace and tranquillity". What he'd overlooked, however, was a further teaching which would benefit leaders and politicians of all nations, the condition that "once we humble ourselves, rid ourselves of our egoism and submit totally in faith and in action, we will surely find peace in our hearts".

It occurred to me that if both sides could find peace in their *hearts* then maybe we could find peace in the *land*. Herzl had himself summed up the true meaning of peace, and whilst he applied it to the Jewish people, it was just as appropriate for the Palestinian Arabs "to live as free men on their own soil, to die peacefully in their own homes".

CHAPTER TWENTY-ONE

Tel Aviv, Israel, 2006

I'm sitting alone in the elegant surroundings of the 24th-floor lounge at Tel Aviv's David Intercontinental Hotel, gazing along the coastline and watching the clear blue waters of the Mediterranean Sea gently wash the sands of Israel. Below me I can look down into the courtyard which forms part of the Hassan Bek Mosque, sitting in isolation in this westernized city dominated by its Jewish population. Across the street remain the ruins of the beachfront discothèque, blown up by a suicide bomber in June 2001, and awaiting an imaginative initiative to bring the site back to life.

Walking along the sea front, I jump out of the way of speeding bicycles, avoid joggers and power-walkers – many of whom seem fitter to drop rather than run – witness elderly men enjoying a challenging and noisy game of backgammon, and mingle with people from a hundred nations. The jabbering is in Hebrew, Arabic, English and Russian as they argue with wild gesticulation, putting the world to rights and seemingly unaware of the continual hooting of impatient drivers on the highway. Here are a people, obstinate, argumentative, occasionally rude and intolerant – mostly on a cell phone – yet determined and vibrant, beautiful and warm.

It's impossible to believe that this is a country engaged in a war which is now well into its second half century since it was established. The laughter of children and teenagers running in and out of the blue waters of the Mediterranean awakens my mind to those children and teenagers just forty miles down the same coast, living in the different environment of the Gaza Strip. What on earth has my generation, our so-called "leaders", Jewish, Arab and Western, done to these youngsters? Aren't they entitled to hope and to have a safe place on earth in which to live, laugh, as well as cry, and enjoy the rays of the sun and peaceful waters of the Mediterranean Sea?

* * *

Theodor Herzl died in 1904. I wonder if he'd be remembered a hundred years later. Would he have been recognized walking down Oxford Street in London, Fifth Avenue in New York or the Champs Elysée in Paris, or even the seafront at Tel Aviv? Was he just a dreamer who had a vision, or a man of huge stature whose legacy was to change the map of the world and write a new chapter of history? Had he lived to a ripe old age, he might have witnessed the birth of the nation he strove to bring to life. Would his power and influence have achieved a Jewish National Home earlier, early enough to have saved six million Jews from one of the great tragedies of history? Would his diplomacy have helped save not only Jewish lives, but also those of the Palestinian Arabs who perished, either defending their homes or seeking to destroy Israel?

Questions, questions, more questions; our lives are full of them, with too few answers. What would Herzl have said and done? He was, after all, a man of action, unafraid to speak his mind in the largest assemblies in Europe and in front of the mightiest and most powerful leaders of the nations?

What did I gain from my many meetings with him? Surely he had said enough to me, planted enough ideas, to make me bold enough to dream about how the tragic conflict centered on such a tiny land sandwiched between the Mediterranean Sea and five unfriendly Arab neighbors might come to a peaceful end.

He wouldn't have been aware of what had occurred in the last sixty years, although he'd have fully understood the animosity and deeply held feelings of the Arabs to the establishment of Israel. As they witnessed waves of immigration, mostly from Europe, they believed that they alone were paying the price for someone else's deeds. The creation of this new state would have confirmed Herzl's vision to establish a sovereign state where Jews could live freely without fear of anti-Semitism from fellow citizens and neighbors, and he fought to obtain a charter which would stand up to international scrutiny and recognition. Sadly this was not to be. Anti-Semitism seems a part of the fabric of history and is on the march yet again, across Europe and beyond, and in one form or another is very much alive. Yet wasn't it this evil which kept the Jewish people united throughout the generations, wasn't it the glue which caused us to "stick together"? It was Herzl himself who said that "anti-Semitism strengthened the sentiment of Jewish solidarity and that Zionism was a homecoming to the Jewish fold even before it became a homecoming to the Jewish land".

I thought I might consider his possible views about the future. I sat quietly in a Jerusalem hotel overlooking the walled old city of King David, the place where history began for the Jews, and where, we're told, Jesus had walked and Muhammad had ascended to heaven.

Little success had resulted from the last half a century as leaders of governments, and particularly those of the United States, had travelled back and forth, endeavoring to mediate between the parties. Even the skills of American secretary of state Henry Kissinger and those like Condoleezza Rice who followed him, failed to ease the tension. Surely it is now time for those who lead the peoples engaged in this struggle for the Holy Land to sit down together, not in Oslo nor Paris, London or Camp David, but on their own doorstep in Tel Aviv, Ramallah or Jerusalem, or a tent in the desert or even a boat on the Mediterranean. *This* is the land over which they struggle – not some grand hotel in Europe or ranch in the United States. The Jews feel under threat from the extreme language and acts of those who seek to destroy them, even before recognizing they exist. This is a people who, having suffered tragedies throughout history, is determined to say "never again will we suffer such anguish", particularly when it is within the memory and personal experience of so many living in Israel today.

In contrast, the Arabs fear the language of those who claim as their right since the days of King Jeroboam, to build their homes in Judea or Samaria on the basis of ancient passages laid down in the Bible. Why, they ask, could the Zionists, and particularly Theodor Herzl and those who supported him, not seek out a piece of land uninhabited – a land without a people, however small it might be – to establish their national home? One might ask the settlers on these disputed lands another question. Surely, alongside the right to live on this historic soil – sits the obligation to measure up to the Hebrew heritage of the Bible, to create a progressive and enlightened society? Perhaps it is these very people, often deeply religious and accused of being extreme in their attitude against their Arab neighbors, who hold the answer to the whole problem. Herzl might well have turned to them to seek a feeling of reconciliation and how they might accept a sharing of land with those whose extreme behavior was proving one of the insurmountable stumbling blocks.

Is it such a terrible thing that the world should protect this one small area of land, merely 20,000 square kilometers, for the Jews to live in peace? Do not the Arabs have masses of land throughout the Middle East in which the Palestinians can live also in peace and tranquillity? But let us not forget that however big the lands are beyond, it is a man's home which is his dominion – and even if it's within a small garden no more than a hundred square meters, be it in Jerusalem or Ramallah, this is where he desires to live, Arab or Jew.

Over and over again the question came back to me. Why cannot these two peoples, with so much to gain from mutual respect and partnership, live together? Surely all they desire is a place on earth in which they can both feel safe? Is it just about land or is it more deeply rooted? If it's land, hasn't a sufficiently high price been paid to establish boundaries between the states? If Israel can withdraw from Gaza after nearly four decades of settlement, then surely it is feasible to draw a boundary which preserves her security and allows the Palestinian Arabs to share the soil of this precious holy land? But perhaps it's more than just land.

The words of Vladimir (Ze'ev) Jabotinsky rushed into my head. The Russian-born journalist, driven by the tragedy of the Russian pogroms to become an active Zionist, said in 1923, "It is impossible to dream of a voluntary agreement between Jew and Arab, not now and not in the foreseeable future. Every nation sees its land as its national home, and wants to stay the sole landlord forever." His views were translated into what he believed to be the only answer: armed conflict. What a tragic prophecy.

Looking at the wider political scene, how can the United States act as honest broker when she is so mistrusted by most of the Arab nations? How can Israel trust the United Nations, who, having given birth has proved so impotent when it came to defending her as a baby and then deserting her when as a teenager she was threatened with extinction?

What might Herzl have counseled or have done in our time? Maybe he'd have recognized the role of the nations of the world whose guiding hand of encouragement was so badly needed and who stood to gain so much from a peaceful and stable Middle East.

Political leadership still maintained a sense of responsibility and a commitment to help sort out the tangle. The powerful United States, who had tried so hard and yet failed; the might of the Russian nation, from where so many Jews had come to Israel and where a modern-day revolution had ended Communism; the influence of Germany, where a tragic period of history had been so painful to the Jews and whose divided country had been so suddenly united by the collapse of the Berlin wall; France, not always the closest friend of Israel, Holland and Belgium whose support for the Jewish people in time of crises was legendary, all had a part to play, as did Great Britain, whose initiative with the Balfour Declaration gave so much heart to the Jews and yet caused so much pain to the Arabs. What about those thirty-three countries who had voted in November 1947 at the United Nations to secure a Jewish state alongside a Palestinian state?

Herzl would have reflected on the decision of Weizmann and Ben-Gurion to accept partition. He would have overlooked the difference between them displayed at the twenty-second Zionist Congress in 1946, meeting in the very same hall at Basel in which he'd organized the first Congress. He knew full well from his own experience that differences between men of passion – some showing moderation, others a lack of patience with the delay in establishing a new country, even its location – generated emotions and harsh words. Most of all, he might well have repeated his journeys of a hundred years earlier across Europe and the Middle East, and this time presented himself with all his powers of persuasion and charisma before the leaders of the opposing Arab nations. Would he not have stood, immaculate as ever, in front of King Abdullah I of Jordan and appealed to his historic friendship and sought an audience with King Farouk of Egypt in the dying days of his monarchy?. He would surely have traveled to Baghdad to remind Crown Prince Abdul Ilah of Iraq that the late father of the boy King Feisal II had signed an agreement with Chaim Weizmann some thirty years earlier conditionally accepting the Balfour Declaration. He would have hoped to achieve the withdrawal of the objection by Iraq's representative, Dr Fadhil Jamail, to the partition plan. And he would have appealed to the modernist King Abdul Aziz to exert the mighty influence of Saudi Arabia.

I doubt Herzl would have stopped there. He would, once again, have used every available day of the closing months of 1947 to travel to London and knock on the door of the British Government to argue the case with foreign secretary Ernest Bevin, and fuel minister Emanuel Shinwell, himself a Jew, who were expressing concern about jeopardizing oil supplies and about Britain's friendship with the Arabs.

Finally, if all this effort failed, Herzl might well have summoned together those nations who demonstrated their confidence in a new young Israel: Australia and New Zealand in the furthest corner of the globe; Uruguay, Ecuador, Peru and Venezuela with almost every nation in the South American continent; Canada and the United States; the supporting countries of Europe from Belgium and France to Russia and Poland, Iceland in the north; South Africa, 33 degrees south of the equator. He would have stood before them, persuading, imploring, even demanding their support for the re-establishment of negotiation and an end to the war, the bitterness and the mistrust, which had wrecked so many lives and caused so many parents to mourn their children.

At the end of the day, he'd have made it clear to the leaders of Israel and the Arabs that the outcome must rest in their own hands. Did he not believe that with all the goodwill of the nations this was a Jewish problem and only the Jews could solve it? He'd have recognized that the price to be paid was high. He would have seen that sacrifices had to be made – land to be given up, Jewish land as well as Arab land, reputations to be damaged and pride to be hurt. He would have sought out the leaders with the courage to break the mold, leaders who would declare that it was time for guns to be stowed and hatred to be set aside. He would have challenged the Israeli and the Arab leadership and demanded of them, "Is this not the real test of leadership of you both, to achieve an agreement with your enemy and turn him into your strongest ally?" What did Herzl say to me when I told him of the unceasing war, "You may have to live in peace with your neighbor without being friends."

Those leaders hold in their hands the lives of their children and grandchildren and the unbelievable opportunities for their future. Consider what Israel has achieved within her own boundaries –converting the barren desert to green and lush pastures where some of the best fruits and vegetables are to be found anywhere in the world. This need not be exclusive to Israel. Imagine the transformation of the neighboring Arab countryside, worked with the united skill and dedication of Arab and Jew, hand in hand with each other. The establishment of a Middle Eastern Economic Community to combat the markets of Europe, the United States and the Orient, providing a quality of life for the Arabs living in Palestine which they couldn't have dreamed of in their own lifetime and which has been denied to so many before. A program of unprecedented building of homes and schools, hospitals and cultural centers, shopping malls and places of entertainment where the peoples of the region would study together, shop together, laugh together, respect each other and, if a miracle happens, *live in peace with each other.*

Both sides of the conflict have young men and women growing up to hate and fear. Entire generations being groomed to fight and ultimately kill either in pursuit of heavenly approval or in the defense of their lives and homes. A culture of destruction, brought to our homes by 24-hour television cameras showing graphic pictures of death and devastation, accompanied by tears and helplessness.

Egypt has embraced peace; Lebanon and Jordan have breathed the air of peace, shattered only by those who occupy their land with one miserable object in life – to destroy Israel. The Gulf States have surely recognized the huge benefits of being free of conflict as they attract investment and tourism on an unprecedented scale. Could not the wealth of Saudi Arabia, home of the Muslim holy cities of Mecca and Medina, not enrich millions of Arab lives by investing in a peaceful future and using their financial strength to reverse the direction of the whole Middle East? Do these states look on from the sidelines with a view that continued conflict is to be encouraged so long as they don't become directly involved? Herzl would ask them to use their combined influence to stop the descent into an unending failure of war and destruction and get behind a new era of peace and mutual understanding.

There must be a key. Which leader has the courage to turn it so that understanding breaks out? Who will suggest the introduction of the largest exchange of young people ever envisaged or attempted? Imagine a hundred or a thousand young Arabs, committed to peace, moved into Israeli homes, changing places and families with a similar number of young Israelis. A period of change of culture and change of life. Could such an imaginative plan produce a better understanding of each other, a respect and ultimately a desire for peace and harmony with all the advantages and happiness that could bring?

A dream and a hope, yes, a dream and a hope. Hope is never lost and a dream is never impossible. Theodor Herzl himself dreamed of a Jewish National Home in Palestine and struggled to achieve it. He couldn't have foreseen the result of his vision and he'd have been distraught by the loss of life, Jewish as well as Arab, and the half century of conflict and hatred which remains the result. And yet I'm convinced he wouldn't have given up, he would have continued to travel and meet leaders, friend or foe, he would have exhausted himself and those around him as he used all of his skill and innovative mind to achieve a Jewish state free of anti-Semitism and at peace with its neighbors.

In 1897 Herzl believed in a two-state answer to the problem. Fifty years later, in 1947, the United Nations in a badly drafted partition plan envisaged the same. Perhaps destiny dictates that this is the only answer. A State of Israel of Jews, and those Arabs and Christians who will commit themselves and their children to a life of peace and prosperity, alongside a State of New Palestine with Arabs who wish to live lives of their own, also committed to peace.

So my dream of meeting Theodor Herzl is at an end. Have I achieved my objective? I am certainly inspired by this man and for all that he stood for. He has inspired generations of Jews with his dream, and now that the Jewish National Home is a reality and Israel faces such challenges, perhaps that inspiration needs to be re-ignited amongst all leaders of the Middle East, Jewish and Arab. He knew that the journey to an ideal society would be long and painful and the fulfillment of his dream rewarding for all who awake to make it come true.

15. *Founding members of the British Younger JNF in Birmingham, England, in 1958, with the author second from left*

16. *The author at a lunch in Jerusalem with Yigael Yadin in 1973*

17. The author with prime minister Golda Meir and Alan Millett at the Churchill Hotel, London, in 1974

18. The author with prime minister Yitzhak Rabin in Birmingham in 1974

19. *The author with refusenik Binyamin Charney in Moscow in 1988*

EPILOGUE - 2017

Salma Khairiya closed her front door and walked through the garden towards the community hall located in the middle of the village. She'd lived in this place for three years and couldn't believe how her life and that of her family had changed, since she moved from Nuseirat, some eight kilometers south of Gaza City. Salma's contentment was only interrupted by the pain which would not leave her heart: the death of her young son, who'd been caught up in the crossfire between Arab and Israeli guns. She had raced to help him, and as she sat at the roadside cradling his body in her arms, he looked up at her with tears in his eyes and pain on his face as his life slowly ebbed away. Her little Fiaz, her pride and joy, whose only crime in life had been to throw a useless stone at an armored car and who couldn't run fast enough to avoid the gunfire between two sworn enemies. Following the trauma of the burial, observed within twenty-four hours by Muslims and Jews alike, Salma had lain in her bed and for two long years cried every night, before falling into a disturbed sleep. Then one morning, she arose and felt an urge in her body she'd not previously experienced. How could members of a nation with the history of the Arab people live in such squalor and without hope? Had her family not lived on this holy soil for generations, and wasn't it as much

213

theirs as anyone else's? It was time to end the crying, dry the tears and look to the future for the sake of her other three children, the memory of Fiaz and the Palestinian Arab people who seemed to be branded as both oppressed and terrorists in the same breath. *There simply must be a better life.*

Some twenty paces down the street, Chava Halevi left her home with a gentle fingertip touch of the mezuza on her door post, as she strolled thoughtfully towards the community center. Her mind raced back to the time she sat on the floor of her kibbutz home, distraught at the news just delivered to her house by an army officer. Her eldest son, Eli, had survived his Gaza assignment – ever fearful of the danger of shooting at the children encouraged to throw missiles. He had been serving with the Israeli army in Lebanon and was reported missing. For days there was a hope, a faint hope, and then came the officer. Eli was dead, killed in action. The whole family were observing the seven days of intense mourning required by Jewish law, as friends and neighbors came to offer sympathy and support. It was of little comfort to Chava, who went to bed every night, her pillow stained from her tears, and for almost two years hardly emerging from her room. One morning she rose and looked closely at her other two children, younger than Eli and just as vibrant and deserving of a better future. And so she thought, *There must be a better life.*

Kfar Salaam veTikva is a picturesque village on a road which reaches Gaza City three miles to the west and some twenty miles to Beersheba in the east. Established in 2017, a century after the Balfour Declaration, following the last Israel/Arab war in Lebanon, which ended in 2006, its population is some 10,000 souls, a mix of Palestinian Arab and Israeli families. Kfar Salaam veTikva, which means "Village of Peace and Hope" in a mixture of Hebrew and Arabic, is the result of another dream. Two mothers, Chava Halevi and Salma Khairiya, were both determined to dedicate their lives to securing a better life and opportunity for their own children, as well as the children of all Palestinians, Arabs and Israelis. Chava and Salma had met by chance, and as their tears mingled together, there came a realization that unless something was done, many more sons would die; many more mothers would mourn, cry and have their hearts broken for the rest of their lives. It is a pain which never goes away.

Salma was born in 1986, the eldest daughter of parents living in the refugee camp of Nuseirat. Her grandparents had fled there from their home in Beersheba, in southern Palestine, following the establishment of the State of Israel. Following eight days of bloody fighting, the Israeli forces had swept into the city, and if only the United Nations had not dithered over the ceasefire decision, the family might still have been in their home. She had childhood memories of stories which told of the despair amongst the Arab population; she was told about the day of her father's birth during the 1956 conflict with Israel following Nasser's nationalization of the Suez Canal, and how Israeli troops had raced across the Sinai Desert. Arriving in Nuseirat, despondency descended over the camp like a dark cloud as they heard about the flight of the Mufti from Gaza to Cairo, and then rumors spread from Egypt that Jordan had agreed to sell refugees to Iraq.

Her grandparents told her how they had lived first in tents and were then transferred to a disused military prison, before being allocated rather inadequate housing. Her grandfather was an honest and intelligent man, a farmer and owner of a modest area of land in the northern Negev of Palestine, before the Jews came. He was hardworking, like his father and grandfather before him, without any enemies, and found it difficult to understand why his whole life had changed because unknown people in a distant land had decided that his country would be divided in half. At first he was happy that his home would be in the Arab part, but when the fighting started and Israel captured the area where he lived, he listened to the community leaders and left for Gaza. He had little or no work, other than occasional laboring across the border, and the family relied on the charity and support of the United Nations.

Sometimes it was enough, most of the time it wasn't, and Nuseirat became a base for young disillusioned Palestinian Arabs who felt cheated and downtrodden. They felt trapped between Israel's unwillingness to accept the return of the refugees and the stubbornness of the Arabs to resettle them. The stories of the past had an impact on Salma who dreamt of the unhappiness and bitterness and dreaded each day as she walked along the road with its open channels of stinking sewage. The last thing she wanted in life was for her children to grow up in such a bitter atmosphere. She asked herself over and over again, why do the children always have to pay such a price for the errors of their parents?

Chava was born in 1977, in Kibbutz Lochamei Hageta'ot, a northern settlement in Israel, founded in 1947 by survivors of the Holocaust in an area facilitated by the Jewish National Fund. Her grandparents, who had emigrated from Poland just before the establishment of the State of Israel, had survived the Chelmno concentration camp where all the members of their families had perished. Seeking the Zionist dream to live in Palestine, they survived the long and dangerous trek across Europe as they took to the boats for the final stage of the journey. Within sight of the Holy Land, their boat was chased by a British naval vessel and a well-paid and competent ship's captain dropped his human cargo on the beach before scuttling away into the night. The initial excitement of the fulfillment of a dream was soon replaced with the reality of a tough life, as her grandparents found the climate too hot and the environment foreign to their European home. Chava's grandfather, who had been a senior lecturer at the university, found agricultural work difficult, although her grandmother had adapted much more quickly to the various duties required by the communal rules of the kibbutz. Throughout their younger days, Chava's parents and family lived in the shadow of the border with Lebanon, which they had regarded for so many years as a friendly neighbor. Her mother had accepted her share of guard duty and led the children to the shelters as the sirens signaled another rocket attack. At times the whole family felt totally isolated from the center of Israel and in the front line of Israel's conflict with the Arabs now that Hizbullah had such influence.

Chava married a kibbutznik and moved to Kfar Giladi just north of Kiryat Shmona, on land owned by the Jewish Colonization Association, established by Baron Hirsch. She and her husband contributed to the growth of the settlement with the births of their children, while under the constant threat of rocket attacks from across the border. She knew the kibbutz members had memories of the attack in 1980 on nearby Misgav Am when three members of the kibbutz, including a child, were killed. When hostilities broke out in 2006 between Israel and Hizbullah, it seemed the world had come crashing down on the kibbutz when twelve soldiers were struck down. Attacks from the air intensified as damage and death descended on the whole of the north of the country. Spasmodic conflict with the Arabs continued and like any mother, Chava felt for those across the border in Lebanon who, during the last war, seemed to be burying their children on a daily basis, as the Israeli army sought out their enemy. And then her world ended. Eli, her eldest son, who had been called up, was reported missing, and as she prayed throughout the night, her prayers brought only an Israeli officer to tell her the news she'd tried to put out of her mind. Eli was no more, his mutilated body recovered from his burned-out tank and returned to his family just to be placed amongst the dust of the earth. She hardly heard the rabbi as he intoned the words intended for those five times his age, "The Lord has given and the Lord has taken away".

Meeting in the community center had become a ritual with all the mothers in Kfar Salaam veTikva. It was beyond belief what had been achieved in this village. Starting with a handful of families, it had grown to thousands and was now facing the problem of insufficient homes and schools for those seeking to relocate there. The village's economy was booming. Shortage of water and competition from other markets had contributed to the decline in orange groves in Israel, but the innovative scheme to draw water from the nearby sea had resulted in the production of the sweetest oranges worldwide. Attracting some of the brightest innovators from the universities of Amman and Beirut and the Weizmann Institute in Rechovot, the Kfar el-Balah School of Advanced Technology was not only providing the young and inquiring minds of the village with a challenging education, but was starting to become an internationally recognized research institution. Arab and Israeli scientists worked together, solving some of the world's food shortage problems, and were establishing relationships with universities across Asia and Africa.

The next day was Friday. The village mosques would be crowded with Muslim worshippers as they welcomed the holy day, and as the sun set, so the Jewish inhabitants headed for the synagogues to welcome the Sabbath. Throughout Kfar Salaam ve-Tikva the dreams of those who had fought for peace were being realized. Muslim and Jewish children played together and against each other. The only confrontation allowed by the village leadership was on the soccer field.

The weekend was to be a special occasion. Visitors were expected from Beirut, Cairo, Jerusalem, Washington and London. Presidents and prime ministers of five countries, together with the newly appointed Secretary General of the United Nations, would visit the village to see exactly how the experiment of an Arab/Israeli joint enterprise was working. A rumor was circulating that the British Government – reflecting on the original commitment of Arthur James Balfour – was proposing that Israel and the adjoining New Palestine State be invited to become members of the British Commonwealth of Nations.

Kfar Salaam veTikva, established in the aftermath of a bloody and disastrous war between Israel and Hizbullah and Hamas, was for a short time the center of international negotiation. The world held its breath. Sitting amongst the shifting sands of the Middle Eastern desert and protected initially by an international force, this tiny haven of peace had demonstrated beyond anyone's expectation that given an opportunity, given a quality of life and successful economy, an ambition and a hope, these two peoples could put away their hate and show the world how respect and tolerance could return to the Holy Land.

Salma Khairiya and Chava Halevi sat in the community center and looked at each other. They had spent many hours discussing how they'd come together, where they had come from, and the dark clouds of war which had hung over an otherwise pleasant land. They'd agreed to put aside their natural feelings of support for either side of the conflict, and try to build a new relationship of mutual respect and understanding. They turned initially to the similarities which could bring Islam and Judaism together – the strict worship of one God, respect for the prophets, a salvation based on good deeds, observance of fasting, and the strength of the family unit. They questioned the rise of extremism in both religions and how much damage it had inflicted on so many generations. The debate followed the dispersal of the Jews and the fall of the Ottoman Empire and how both events had left their peoples without a home, and subject to oppression and exploitation. More recently, the repeated victories of Israel over the Arab armies had left a feeling of inadequacy and deep sense of loss of honor. It was inevitable that their conversation turned to the most recent war which had spread over some thirty-four days between Israel and Hizbullah in southern Lebanon. Had this conflict changed the course of history? The Arabs had experienced many charismatic leaders in the last fifty years, but almost all had been losers. The rise of Hassan Nasrallah, the leader of Hizbullah, had brought not just charisma, but a perceived winner. Salma found a natural identification with him because not only had he dragged himself out of the poverty of Eastern Beirut but he too had lost his eldest son to an Israeli bullet. Whilst this personal pain, as well as his strict Shi'ite upbringing and deep feeling of hate for Israel, had driven Nasrallah to strike back at what he saw as the conquerors, Salma felt the time was ripe for a new kind of Arab leadership which would bring peace to the land.

Meanwhile, Chava could not forget the soul searching and acrimony which had spread throughout the State of Israel following the 2006 Lebanon War. Criticism of the military, attacks on the government, and doubts about the intelligence had filled the pages of the press and television screens. Israel's fighting machine, its self-styled defense force, was seen for the very first time in Israel's history to have failed. But, she had asked herself over and over again, was this really true, and perhaps this was not failure, but an opportunity to change everything in the Middle East?

Despite all of this soul searching, Salma and Chava still had tears in their eyes as they recalled their two sons, Fiaz and Eli, whose young lives had ended suddenly along with so many others before they could fully breathe the air of life and happiness. They reached out to each other as they moved to the window to look out on what they'd started. Together they realized that perhaps the agony and the pain – which would never fully leave their hearts – had not been completely in vain. Sixty years of war and destruction were now being exchanged for a new era for their peoples. Were not Salma and Chava descended from the same father millennia ago, were they not both victims of history, and how often did children of the same parents live side by side without really liking each other?

The arrival of their distinguished guests was not just a tribute to their struggle and eventual success in establishing Kfar Salaam veTikva, it was the recognition that people of integrity with strength of character could overcome prejudice and hate. Now, it was time for leaders to lead in the paths of peace and reconciliation.

Theodor Herzl dreamed of a Jewish National Home. Others had dreamed of a home for the Palestinian people. When history began, a tiny country was established at the crossroads of the world, bridging the cultures of east and west – Palestine, a country divided by prejudice, united by destiny and at war with itself. Two great biblical nations facing each other with passion and pride out of which was born a pain, the pain of survival. Was it so inconceivable that the two could live side by side in peace or was that just another dream? Salma Khairiya and Chava Halevi certainly believed it was no dream. And wasn't it Theodor Herzl himself who said, "If you will it, it is no dream…"?

END

BIBLIOGRAPHY

Bein, Alex (1943) *Theodore Herzl – a Biography*, Jewish Publication Society

Beller, Steven (2004) *Herzl*, Peter Halban

Ben-Gurion, David, et al. (1962) *Chaim Weizmann*, Weidenfield & Nicolson

Brenner, Michael (2003) *Zionism – A brief History*, Markus Wiener

Edelman, Michael (1964) *Ben Gurion*, Hodder & Stoughton

Gilbert, Martin (1998) *Israel – A History*, Doubleday/Black Swan

Johnson, Paul (1987) *A History of the Jews*, Weidenfeld & Nicolson

Keller, Werner (1971) *Diaspora*, Pitman

Klegg and Guttman (1997) *Kunsthalle Basel*

Lewis, Bernard (2002) *What Went Wrong*, Weidenfeld & Nicolson

Lowenthal, Marvin (1956) *The Diaries of Theodor Herzl*, The Dial Press

Rubinstein, Amnon (2000) *From Herzl to Rabin*, Holmes & Meier

Sacharov, Eliyahu (2004) *Out of the Limelight*, Gefen

Stewart, Desmond (1974) *Theodor Herzl*, Hamish Hamilton

INDEX